KU-329-280

MAINSTREAMING REPORT

PROPOUND – Developing a Key Competences Model for University Postgraduate Programmes
MAINSTREAMING REPORT

Junio 2013

Depósito Legal: 978-84-15873-08-2
ISBN: Gr-1285/2013

Edición e Impresión: Godel Impresiones Digitales S.L.

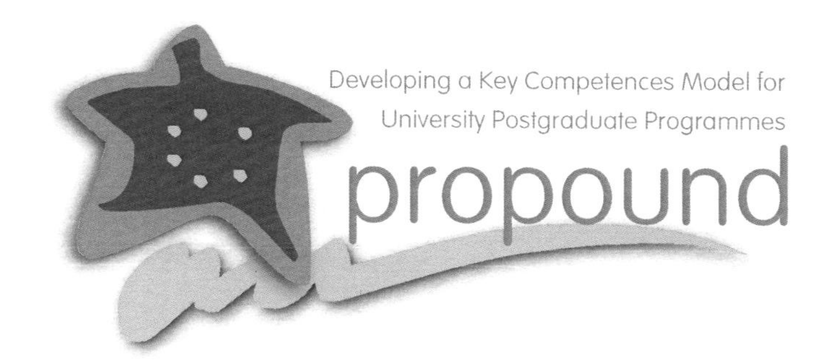

TABLE OF CONTENTS

1. Introduction ... 7
2. European Policy, Institutional and Legal Context ... 11
2.1. Policy Context: Lisbon Declaration and European Strategy 2020 ... 11
2.2. Institutional Context: the Modernization Agenda for European Universities ... 13
2.3. The Legal Context: the decisions and laws related to key competences ... 16
2.3.1. The European Qualifications Framework for Lifelong Learning ... 16

2.4. What can we learn from other international contexts? 17
2.4.1. Moldova – a case study for Eastern Europe 17
2.4.2. USA – Future Work Skills 2020: Skills for the Future Workforce 18
2.4.3. 21st Century Skills: Learning for Life in our Times 18
3. Conceptualization of Key Competences 19
3.1. The OECD key competences framework 19
3.2 The EU Key Competences framework 20
4 Key competences and employability of postgraduates in Europe 23
4.1. Key Competences and socio-economic development in Europe 20
4.2. Higher Education Attainment 24
4.3. Employability 24
4.4. Unemployment 26
5. National Policy Contexts 31
5.1. United Kingdom 31
5.1.1. National Policy 31
5.1.2. But does it work? 32
5.1.3. Current developments 32
5.2. Spain 33
5.2.1. National Policy Context 33
5.3. Italy 34
5.3.1. National policy 34
5.3.2. Focus on access and transition 35
5.4. The Netherlands 36
5.4.1. Dutch policy for curricular reform in higher education 36
5.4.2. Focus on access and transition 36
5.5. Estonia 37
6. The PROPOUND Project 41
6.1. Recognition of Key Competences 41
6.1.1. Two possible routes for key competences formal recognition 43
6.1.2. Conclusion 45
6.2. Assessment Methodologies for Key Competences 45
6.2.1. Concept of Assessment of Key Competences 46
6.2.2. Current issues in the assessment of key competences 46
6.2.3. Challenges in the assessment of key competences 46
6.2.4. Preconditions for the assessment of key competences: the articulation of learning outcomes 46
6.2.5. Overview of valuable examples in assessment of key competences at University level 47
6.2.6. E-assessment 49
6.2.7. Conclusion 49
6.3. Teaching and Learning 49
6.3.1. Graduate Attributes Approach 49
6.3.2. Graduate Competency Building 50
6.3.3. Work-based learning 50
6.3.4. Skills Workshops 51
6.3.5. Blended and Online Teaching Approach 51
6.3.6. Professional Development Portfolio Methods 52
6.3.7. Conclusion 53
6.4. Training the Trainers and Assessors 53
6.4.1. Requirements for the trainer of assessors Besides controlling the aforementioned skills, the trainer of assessors needs to be able to function in different roles: 53
6.4.2. The competences of the assessor 55
6.4.3. Design of the assessor training 55
7. Implications for Higher Education, Employers and Policy Makers 57
7.1. HE facing the learner's claim for fame 57
7.2. Integrating key competences in learning outcomes 59
7.3. For Employers 60
7.4. For Policy Makers 62
7.4.1. Education to Employment - Designing a system that works 62
8. Conclusions 65

MAINSTREAMING REPORT

>

INTRODUCTION

Chapter 1

Introduction

The PROPOUND Project - Developing a Key Competences Model for University Postgraduate Programmes – is supported by the EU Lifelong Learning Programme with a project consortium of two universities, two higher education foundations, three businesses and a national qualifications authority, led by the Fundación General Universidad de Granada Empresa.

The main objective of the PROPOUND project is to drive the modernisation agenda of universities, promoting curricular reforms directed to improve the employability potential of postgraduate students. The project aims to encourage dialogue and cooperation between universities and enterprises for the exchange and design of innovative curricular strategies and tools in postgraduate programmes that would better respond to the labour market needs and promote the development, assessment and certification of key competences of the postgraduate students.

The project aims to develop, experiment with and validate different methodologies of identification and evaluation of key competences in the postgraduate programmes in Spain, Italy, Netherlands, UK and Estonia.

Key competences are those non-disciplinary or transversal competences critical to employability and employment skills. They are defined at national level in various ways and at European level by a Framework of eight Key Competences:

Table 1. European Framework of Key Competences for Lifelong Learning.

	Competences
1	Communication in the mother longue
2	Communication in foreign languages
3	Mathematical competence and basic competences in science and technology
4	Digital competence
5	Learning to learn
6	Social and civic competences
7	Sense of initiative and entrepreneurship
8	Cultural awareness and expression

Source: Key Competences for Lifelong Learning. European Reference Framework.

This project is extremely timely because of the continuing economic and employment crisis in Europe. Unemployment rates have increased, especially in Southern Europe, and youth unemployment including graduates and post-graduates has risen to unacceptable levels in some countries. At the same time, employers continue to complain about skills shortages and especially the employability of graduates and post-graduates.

The PROPOUND project provides an improved understanding of this phenomena, together with a set of remedies to assist European universities to respond by building key competences more structurally into their post-graduate programs.

In light of this, pilot projects have been completed is each of the partner countries whereby:

In Spain, the pilot incorporates a model of assessment and development of key competences in a Master Programme **in 3D Animation of Characters** at the University of Granada. The model is experimented through an internship period of students at a national animation firm (Kandor Graphics) with a focus on assessment of key competences in the informal learning context (work experience) and emphasis in the self-management of competences by the postgraduate students. The main objectives of the Pilot Action are to answer to the needs of the current Spanish labour market and the European Higher Education Area in the development of the key competences for employability; and to support postgraduate students to identify the key competences that can be acquire through internship work experience

In the U.K., the pilot programme explores through interviews and focus groups the experience of learners in the selected programmes in respect of the development, evidencing and assessment of the essential knowledge, skills and attitudes associated with ***Learning to Learn***. In particular, the pilot attempts to identify the scope for learner self-assessment as a means of securing active learner engagement and entails a **survey** of full-time students on 12 month Masters programmes with students being a mixture of UK, European and international (non-EU). A **focus group** of five recently graduated Masters students also comprises part of the pilot as well as an **analysis** of degree programme **documentation** of the University of Edinburgh.

In Estonia, the pilot investigates how ***communication competence*** could be developed and assessed directly as one of the expected learning outcomes across three postgraduate degree programmes at Estonian Business School. Testing the pilot involved developing appropriate assessment criteria to the corresponding learning outcome, developing appropriate assessment methods, and testing the designed tools.

In the Netherlands, the pilot involved an up streaming programme for teacher training. A process for the Accreditation of Prior Learning (APL) of the competences of trainers (as assessors) was used involving counselling methods, portfolio assessment and criteria based interviews. Based on this, appropriate training and certification of assessors was carried out.

In Italy, the pilot explored the extent to which Key Competences are fostered within University postgraduate programmes and how acquainted students are with them. The pilot focussed on surveying (via self-assessment questionnaires) the Key Competences that students already possess and are able to recognise by themselves; and identify how they have developed these, either through University or their personal social lives.

Further details and descriptions of the activities of the project can be found in the Preliminary Report.

The purpose of this report is to assist and support higher education institutions in devising and implementing curricula design changes, with related management and governance arrangements, to support the identification, development and validation of key competences among postgraduate students.

The report is structured as follows:

Chapter 2: provides an overview of the supranational policy context in terms of the agenda in Europe for social and economic development and the modernisation of higher education. A brief commentary on the policy frameworks for transversal key competences from outside the EU is also provided here.

Chapter 3: explores the basic concepts for an overall understanding of skills and competences, their transferability and an overview of the existing European framework.

Chapter 4: gives a snapshot of current evidence of postgraduate educational attainment, Key Competences and employment across Europe.

Chapter 5: outlines the main national policy imperatives relevant to transversal key competences in higher education in the countries represented in the project.

Chapter 6: provides a summary of the key findings of the PROPOUND project activities. This chapter provides a discussion of the main issues in curricula reform to promote the adoption and uptake of transversal Key Competences in higher education in Europe. These include how Key Competences can be recognised within or alongside formal curricula; approaches to the teaching, learning and assessing Key Competences to promote the employability of postgraduate students, and the consideration of staff development needs to support implementation of Key Competences in European universities.

Chapter 7: is about how to effect these radical changes to the planning, teaching, learning and assessment of key competences in postgraduate courses.

This report feeds in to an Action Plan framework to support higher education providers in implementing curricula reform based on Key Competences.

EUROPEAN POLICY, INSTITUTIONAL AND LEGAL CONTEXT

Chapter 2

European Policy, Institutional and Legal Context

2.1. Policy Context: Lisbon Declaration and European Strategy 2020

In terms of content, the most crucial phase in the European integration process having a major impact on developments in the Higher Education and research policy is **the "Lisbon Declaration"** which began in 2000[1]. At their Lisbon meeting, EU leaders decided on a process to boost the Union's competitiveness and growth. The aim was *to create a Europe of knowledge* and formulated the goal that, by 2010, the EU should have been *the most competitive and dynamic knowledge-based economy in the world, capable of sustainable economic growth, with more and better jobs, and greater social cohesion*.

In response to the concerns expressed at the Lisbon European Council on 23 and 24 March 2000, the policies related to education and basic skills proved to be essential pillars to create a knowledge-based economy. It was considered that the **development of key competences would provide added value for employment and social cohesion by guaranteeing more flexibility in the labour force,** allowing it to adapt more quickly to constant changes and contributing to the motivation and satisfaction of workers and the quality of work.

In the same direction, on the one side, the Framework of Actions for the Lifelong Development of Competences and Qualifications, adopted by the European social partners in March 2002[2], emphasized the need for businesses to adapt their structures more quickly in order to remain innovative, productive and competitive and evolve towards learning organisations. Therefore, the ability of organisations to identify competences, to mobilise and recognise them and to encourage their development for all employees represented the basis for renewed human resources strategies.

1 See European Council 23 and 24 March 2000, Presidency Conclusions at: http://www.europarl.europa.eu/summits/lis1_en.htm on the Lisbon Declaration.

2 ETUC, UNICE, and CEEP (2002) *Framework of Actions for the Lifelong Development of Competences and Qualifications*. See. http://www.etuc.org/a/580.

On the other side, the **Report of the Employment Taskforce issued in 2003**[3] stressed the role of education and lifelong learning in the strengthening of social cohesion and the importance of key competences for personal fulfilment and development, social inclusion, active citizenship and employability.

To meet the needs of the wider employment market, **EU Universities** have had to face the challenge of strengthening the employability potential of their young highly qualified graduates by improving educational attainment levels and by introducing necessary key competences in curricular programmes. This aspect has also been reflected at the intergovernmental level by the Bologna Process.

Since then, those conclusions have been regularly restated including by the Brussels European Councils (March 2003, December 2003 and March 2005),and in **the Integrated Guidelines for Growth and Jobs 2005-2008, approved by the June 2005 European Council**[4] that re-launched the Lisbon Declaration. In particular, the Employment Guidelines call for education and training systems to be adapted in response to new competence requirements through better identification of occupational needs and key competences as part of Member States' reform programmes.

In order to support and provide Member States with a reference tool for the provision of key competences for lifelong learning, the European Parliament and the Council issued the **Recommendation on Key Competences for Lifelong Learning (December 2006)**[5]**.** The EU addressed the key competences for employability, creativity and innovation through eight **Key Competences Framework for Lifelong Learning**: "communication in the mother tongue", "communication in foreign languages", "mathematical competence and basic competences in science and technology", "digital competence", "learning to learn", "a sense of initiative and entrepreneurship", "social and civic competences" and "cultural awareness".

In line with the objectives of **the Education and Training 2010 work programme, adopted in 2004**[6]**,** this reference framework built on the basis for action at Community level, and was addressed to encourage national and European efforts of policy makers, education and training providers, employers and learners and to facilitate national reforms and further cooperation between Member States.

From this renewed stand point, the Commission recommended that Member States use the Framework as a reference in the implementation of the European initiatives of **New Skills for New Jobs (2009)**[7]and **Youth on the Move (2010)**[8] with support from the **Community education and training programmes** such as the integrated LLP programme (2007-2013) or related Community policies (employment, youth, cultural and social policies) and ensure that these programmes promote the acquisition of key competences at all levels, including in higher education.

In fact, as a consequence of the current economic crisis and the considerable increase of youth unemployment across Europe1, a new migration phenomenon is taking force in the young graduate population. Thus, these flagship initiatives and programmes make particular emphasis on the need to

3 European Employment Taskforce (2003) ***Jobs, jobs, jobs – creating more employment in Europe*** EET.
4 European Council (2005) Decision 2005/ 600/ EC.
5 European Parliament & Council. (2006) Recommendation 2006/962/EC.
6 European Council (2004). 6905/04. 3 March.
7 European Commission (2009) ***New Skills for New Jobs: anticipating and matching labour market and skills needs.*** European Commission, April.
8 See http://ec.europa.eu/news/culture/100915_2_en.htm

invest at all levels in mobility and foreign languages, by encouraging more students to take advantage of EU grants to study or go for traineeships abroad in order to improve young people's skills to adapt to different cultural contexts and match the demands of the labour market.

And last but not least, the renewed **Strategy Europe 2020**[9] aimed to *achieve smart, sustainable and inclusive growth in the EU* by investing in human capital, promoting personal fulfilment, social cohesion and active citizenship, creativity and innovation, including entrepreneurship, follows that stated in the **strategic framework for European cooperation in education and training, Education and Training 2020**[10]**,** which leverages lifelong learning and mobility orientated policies to meet the socio-economic and demographic challenges already mentioned. Both strategies place again an increased attention on the take up of developing key competences at European, national and local levels.

And finally, a **Grand Coalition** on e-skills[11], reflecting the fourth key competence, was inaugurated in Brussels on 4 and 5 March 2013, by the President of the Commission, both Vice-Presidents, two other Commissioners, and the Irish Presidency, with participation by two partners of this PROPOUND project.

Despite this wealth of policies, processes and strategies, the European Key Competences Framework remains largely unknown and unimplemented in most European universities.

9 See http://ec.europa.eu/europe2020/index_en.htm

10 http://ec.europa.eu/education/lifelong-learning-policy/framework_en.htm

11 See http://ec.europa.eu/digital-agenda/en/grand-coalition-digital-jobs-0

2.2. Institutional Context: the Modernization Agenda for European Universities

The role of HE in the knowledge society is fully recognized in the EU strategy for smart, inclusive and sustainable growth. It is associated with supporting innovation through a more effective knowledge triangle as well as **preparing a highly qualified workforce with the competences needed in evolving labour markets**. This relates to a complex and increasingly flexible economic model requiring advanced competences but also to full investment in human potential to innovate at economic, social and political level.

The European policy framework and priority setting in the Higher Education area is given by the intertwined action of the **Bologna Process** and the **Modernization Agenda of the European Commission**[12], within the overarching objective of implementing lifelong learning in Europe.

The Bologna Process – initiated at the end of the 90s as an intergovernmental process - aims to create a European Higher Education Area (EHEA)[13], intended as an open education environment favouring full mobility of students and staff, through transparency, recognition and a shared commitment to quality.

The modernization agenda – coming for the European Commission – aims to unfold the potential of HE in Europe to match the challenges of the knowledge society, supporting innovation and growth through excellence in research and teaching, by tackling the need for advanced competences and highly skilled human resources. Currently its specific objectives include to:

12 See http://ec.europa.eu/education/higher-education/agenda_en.htm

13 See http://www.ehea.info/

- Increase the quantity of higher education graduates at all levels.
- Enhance the quality and relevance of human capital development in higher education.
- Create effective governance and funding mechanisms in support of excellence and strengthen the knowledge triangle between education, research and business.

In both initiatives, enhancing the relevance of higher education to society and the labour market is a crucial concern – associated with employability, innovation and democratic participation – and developing "competences" beyond knowledge and skills is a key mission of higher education.

While transversal competences do not yet feature among the "flagships" of the Bologna Process and the Modernization Agenda, substantial work is being doing at European level to support approaches which move from learning input to learning outcomes in HE. Starting with the need to enhance transparency and recognition among systems, such effort has substantially concentrated on supporting a more competence-based approach in Higher Education as part of a strategy to enhance HE relevance to society and reduce mismatch in the labour market.

Substantial contribution in this area has been given by the TUNING project[14] which has been working incrementally to support transparency and quality of HE programmes in Europe. With respect to the necessary competences to be developed by HE, TUNING has acknowledged the importance of what it calls "generic competences" and transferable skills. Tuning distinguishes three types of generic competences:

- Instrumental competences: cognitive abilities, methodological abilities, technological abilities and linguistic abilities.
- Interpersonal competences: individual abilities like social skills (social interaction and co-operation).
- Systemic competences: abilities and skills concerning whole systems (combination of understanding, sensibility and knowledge; prior acquisition of instrumental and interpersonal competences required).

Table 2. TUNING Project. Generic Competences

TUNNING Project: Generic Competences	
Capacity for analysis and synthesis	Problem solving Decision-making
Capacity for applying knowledge in practice	Teamwork
Planning and time management	Interpersonal skills
Basic general knowledge in the field of study	Leadership
Grounding in basic knowledge of the profession in practice	Ability to work in an interdisciplinary team
Oral and written communication in your native language	Ability to communicate with non-experts (in the field)
Knowledge of a second language	Appreciation of diversity and the multicultural aspect
Elementary computing skills	Ability to wok in an international context
Research skills	Understanding of cultures and customs of other countries
Capacity to learn	Ability to work autonomously
Information management skills (ablitily to retrieve from different sources)	Project design and management
Critical and self-critical abilities	Initiative and entrepreneurial spirit
Capacity to adapt to new situations	Ethical commitment
Capacity for generating new ideas (creativity)	Concern for quality
	Will to succeed

Source: TUNING Project (www.unideusto.org/tuning/).

Despite increasing attention to the "key competences" issue at HE level, still progress is perceived

14 See http://www.unideusto.org/tuning/

as slow with respect to the overarching objectives of Europe with respect to higher education.

In its 2011 Communication "Supporting growth and jobs – an agenda for the modernization of Europe's higher education systems"[15], the European Commission stresses that "**the potential of European higher education institutions to fulfill their role in society and contribute to Europe's prosperity remains underexploited"** and insists explicitly on the need that HE provide people with the "right mix of skills" for the knowledge economy, including transversal competences, e-skills for the digital era, creativity and flexibility and a solid understanding of their chosen field (such as in Science, Technology, Engineering and Maths). While these competences are essential, public and private employers, including in research intensive sectors, increasingly report mismatches and difficulties in finding the right people for their evolving needs.

The modernization agenda invites the EU and member states to work to enhance the quality and relevance of their HE systems for instance by involving more employers and labour market actors as well as fully exploiting the potential of ICT to support more effective learning.

A set of important tools developed at EU levels to support HE reform now offers the framework to move towards increasing focus on key competences in university learning. This is the case in particular of the European Qualifications Framework (EQF), and – as specifically concerns HE – the European Credit Transfer System (ECTS) and the **overarching framework for qualifications in the EHEA**, described in generic learning outcomes associated to each level (the so-called "Dublin Descriptors[16]**") and corresponding to a number of ECTS credits.**

15 COM(2011) 567 final.
16 See http://www.jointquality.nl/content/descriptors/CompletesetDublinDescriptors.doc

Specifically, the Dublin Descriptors offer a general description of the typical expectations for success and connected skills with the definitive degrees in the three cycles of Bologna.

These descriptors are formulated on the basis of five dimensions and are to be interpreted in relationship to one another:

- Knowledge and understanding.
- Practical application of knowledge and understanding.
- Making judgments.
- Communicative skill
- Autonomous learning skills.

Expected Learning Outcomes (LOs) are defined on the basis of these dimensions at the end of each cycle of study. Such formulation offers scope to integrate transversal skills as expected outcomes of Higher Education provided that these are conceived as integrated with "hard" skills and knowledge rather than in their "isolated" understanding.

By integrating the dimension of LOs, the ECTS is now becoming more effective in enhancing transparency, recognition and mobility, by expressing workload associated to the achievement of specific LOs.

The focus on LOs and competences highlights the coming of a substantial change in the teacher/learning paradigm in which student-centered approaches are becoming ever more important. The need to value and recognize learning has an impact on the appraisal and construction of degree-granting educational programs as they move from a teacher-centered educational system to one centered on learning.

Here the centrality of the concept of competency emerges. The previous paradigm placed emphasis on the transmission and acquisition of knowledge. In this new paradigm shift there are a number of elements involved: student-centered education, different roles of the teacher, redefinition of objectives, a change in the approach to educational activity, a shift of the emphasis from input to output and a change in the organization of learning.

2.3. The Legal Context: the decisions and laws related to key competences

2.3.1. The European Qualifications Framework for Lifelong Learning

The European Qualifications Framework for Lifelong Learning (EQF) was adopted by the European Parliament and Council on 23 April 2008. The EQF is a common European reference framework acting as a translation device to make qualifications more readable and understandable across different countries and systems in Europe. It has two principal aims: to promote citizens' mobility between countries and to facilitate their lifelong learning.

The EQF is a two-dimensional competence framework describing eight levels of competence (qualifications) in terms of three descriptors:

- Knowledge.
- Skills.
- Autonomy and responsibility (competence).

The Communiqué of the Conference of European Ministers Responsible for Higher Education, Bergen, 19-20 May 2005, is an important milestone in developing the European Higher Education Area (EHEA). The ministers declare:

We adopt the overarching framework for qualifications in the EHEA, comprising three cycles (including, within national contexts, the possibility of intermediate qualifications), generic descriptors for each cycle based on learning outcomes and competences, and credit ranges in the first and second cycles.

We commit ourselves to elaborating national frameworks for qualifications compatible with the overarching framework for qualifications in the EHEA by 2010, and to having started work on this by 2007. We ask the Follow-up Group to report on the implementation and further development of the overarching framework.

We underline the importance of ensuring complementarity between the overarching framework for the EHEA and the proposed broader framework for qualifications for lifelong learning[17] encompassing general education as well as vocational education and training as now being developed within the European Union as well as among participating countries.

Generic descriptors for each cycle based on learning outcomes are provided by the so called Dublin Descriptors. The Dublin Descriptors[18] provide very general statements of typical expectations of achievements and abilities associated with awards that represent the end of a Bologna cycle. General level descriptors have been developed for the 'short cycle within the first cycle' and the first, second and third cycle.

The descriptors consist of a set of criteria, phrased in terms of competence levels, which enables to distinguish in a broad and general manner

17 Reference is made to the EQF, which has not been adopted yet in 2005.

18 http://www.jointquality.nl/content/descriptors/Completeset-DublinDescriptors.doc

between the different cycles. The following five sets of criteria are distinguished:

- Acquiring knowledge and understanding.
- Applying knowledge and understanding.
- Making informed judgements and choices.
- Communicating knowledge and understanding.
- Capacities to continue learning.

On 18 December 2006 the European Parliament and the Council adopted a **Recommendation on Key Competences for Lifelong Learning** (cf. p.3)[19]. The key competences form part of the objectives of the Education and Training 2010 work programme, the Commission communication on making a European area of lifelong learning a reality. The Recommendation stipulates that key competences should be acquired by:

- Young people at the end of their compulsory education and training, equipping them for adult life, particularly for working life, whilst forming a basis for further learning.
- Adults throughout their lives, through a process of developing and updating skills.

The Key Competences framework is a reference tool for EU countries and their education and training policies. EU countries should try to ensure:

- That initial education and training offer all young people the means to develop the key competences to a level that equips them for adult and working life, thus also providing a basis for future learning.
- That appropriate provision is made for young people who are disadvantaged in their training so that they can fulfil their educational potential.
- That adults can develop and update key competences throughout their lives, particularly priority target groups such as persons who need to update their competences.
- That appropriate infrastructure is in place for continuing education and training of adults, that there are measures to ensure access to education and training and the labour market and that there is support for learners depending on their specific needs and competences.
- The coherence of adult education and training provision through close links between the policies concerned.

19 European Parliament and Council (2006) Recommendation 2006/962/EC.

2.4. What can we learn from other international contexts?

2.4.1. Moldova – a case study for Eastern Europe

Moldova is a small country on the eastern fringe of Europe, between Romania and Ukraine. Its economy used to be integrated with the Soviet Union, but those markets have been lost. The country is attempting to develop new markets in Europe.

A critical issue is the shortage of appropriate skills. Employers complain strongly that the universities are not producing the graduates and postgraduates that the country needs. They especially complain about poor transverse skills such as:

- Modern European languages, most especially English.
- Communications.
- Team work.

- Business understanding.
- Project management.

Moldova is a member of the EHEA and has largely implemented the three cycle degree structure of Bologna, and has made some progress on implementing LOs.

But other aspects of Bologna are not well understood, and progress has been slow:

- Curricula reform (much of which remains rooted in the Soviet tradition).
- University - employer engagement, e.g. in Senate, external examiners.
- Quality assurance, both internal and external.
- Modern teaching, learning and assessment methods.

Moldova needs assistance from its regional neighbours and from Europe generally.

2.4.2. USA – Future Work Skills 2020: Skills for the Future Workforce

In 2011, the University of Phoenix Research Institute published a report, listed in UNESCO, entitled: Future Work Skills 2020[20] which identifies six drivers, affecting future workforces. These are: extreme longevity; rise of smart machines and systems; new media ecology; computation world, super structured organisations and a globally connected world. In light of these, the report then defines ten ***Skills for the Future Workforce***: Sense-making; Social intelligence; Novel and adaptive thinking; Cross -cultural competency; Computational thinking; New-media literacy; Trans-disciplinarity; Design mindset; Cognitive load management; and Virtual collaboration.

20 Institute for the Future & University of Phoenix Research Institute (2011) *Future Workskills: 2020.* IFTF/ UoP.

This is one research outcome, but it seems likely that others will follow similarly.

2.4.3. 21st Century Skills: Learning for Life in our Times

The *Partnership for 21st Century Skills*[21] is a US-based organisation that proposes elements described as "21st century student outcomes" which are the skills, knowledge and expertise needed for learning for life in our times in order to succeed. These skills are clustered into three groups as Learning & Innovation Skills; Digital Literacy Skills (Information, Media and Technology); Life and Career Skills.

We must consider how such theories and empirical studies will go on to influence future competences for postgraduates entering and competing in labour markets.

21 Trilling, B. & Fadel, C. (2012) *21st Century Skills: learning for life in our times.* Jossey Bass.

Chapter 3

Conceptualization of Key Competences

Key Competences[1] are those of particular value, that have multiple areas of usefulness and that are needed by everyone[2].

The first of these conditions, that competences should be valued, applies in relation to measurable benefits for both economic and social purposes. Recent research reinforces the view that human capital not only plays a critical role in economic performance, but also brings key individual and social benefits such as better health, improved wellbeing, better parenting, and increased social and political engagement.

The second condition, that competences should bring benefits in a wide spectrum of contexts, means that they should apply to multiple areas of life. Thus, certain areas of competence are needed not only in the labour market but also in private relationships, in political engagement and so on, and it is these transversal competencies that are defined as key.

The third condition, that key competences should be important for all individuals, deemphasises those competences that are of use only in a specific trade, occupation or walk of life. Emphasis is given to transversal (key) competences that everyone should aspire to develop and maintain.

3.1. The OECD key competences framework

The **key competences framework developed by the OECD** includes nine key competences grouped into three competence categories.

Competence category 1: **Using Tools Interactively** is important, because of:

- The need to keep up to date with technologies.
- The need to adapt tools to own purposes.

1 **Competence** means the proven ability to use knowledge, skills and personal, social and/or methodological abilities, in work or study situations and in professional and personal development.
2 See http://www.oecd.org/pisa/35070367.pdf

- The need to conduct active dialogue with the world.

Competence category 1 includes 3 competences:

- Use language, symbols and texts interactively.
- Use knowledge and information interactively.
- Use technology interactively.

Competence category 2: **Interacting in Heterogeneous Groups** is important, because of:

- The need to deal with diversity in pluralistic societies.
- The importance of empathy.
- The importance of social capital.

Competence category 2 includes 3 competences:

- Relate well to others.
- Co-operate, work in teams.
- Manage and resolve conflicts.

Competence category 3: **Acting Autonomously** is important, because of:

- The need to realise one's identity and set goals, in complex world.
- The need to exercise rights and take responsibility.
- The need to understand one's environment and its functioning.

Competence category 3 includes 3 competences:

- Act within the big picture.
- Form and conduct life plans and personal projects.
- Defend and assert rights, interests, limits and needs.

3.2. The EU Key Competences framework

The EU key competences for lifelong learning are a combination of **knowledge, skills and attitudes**[3] appropriate to the context. They are particularly necessary for personal fulfilment and development, social inclusion, active citizenship and employment. They provide also added value by offering flexibility and adaptability, satisfaction and motivation.

The key competences framework defines **eight key competences** and describes the essential knowledge, skills and attitudes related to each of these:

- **Communication in the mother tongue**, which is the ability to express and interpret concepts, thoughts, feelings, facts and opinions in both oral and written form (listening, speaking, reading and writing) and to interact linguistically in an appropriate and creative way in a full range of societal and cultural contexts.
- **Communication in foreign languages**, which involves, in addition to the main skill dimensions of communication in the mother tongue, mediation and intercultural understanding. The level of proficiency depends on

3 For the definitions of knowledge, skills and attitudes, please see the Recommendation at: http://europa.eu/legislation_summaries/education_training_youth/lifelong_learning/c11090_en.htm

several factors and the capacity for listening, speaking, reading and writing.

- **Mathematical competence and basic competences in science and technology**. Mathematical competence is the ability to develop and apply mathematical thinking in order to solve a range of problems in everyday situations, with the emphasis being placed on process, activity and knowledge. Basic competences in science and technology refer to the mastery, use and application of knowledge and methodologies that explain the natural world. These involve an understanding of the changes caused by human activity and the responsibility of each individual as a citizen.

- **Digital competence** involves the confident and critical use of information society technology and thus basic skills in information and communication technology (ICT).

- **Learning to learn** is related to learning, the ability to pursue and organise one's own learning, either individually or in groups, in accordance with one's own needs, and awareness of methods and opportunities.

- **Social and civic competences**. Social competence refers to personal, interpersonal and intercultural competence and all forms of behaviour that equip individuals to participate in an effective and constructive way in social and working life. It is linked to personal and social well-being. An understanding of codes of conduct and customs in the different environments in which individuals operate is essential. Civic competence, and particularly knowledge of social and political concepts and structures (democracy, justice, equality, citizenship and civil rights), equips individuals to engage in active and democratic participation.

- **Sense of initiative and entrepreneurship** is the ability to turn ideas into action. It involves creativity, innovation and risk-taking, as well as the ability to plan and manage projects in order to achieve objectives. The individual is aware of the context of his/her work and is able to seize opportunities that arise. It is the foundation for acquiring more specific skills and knowledge needed by those establishing or contributing to social or commercial activity. This should include awareness of ethical values and promote good governance.

- **Cultural awareness and expression**, which involves appreciation of the importance of the creative expression of ideas, experiences and emotions in a range of media (music, performing arts, literature and the visual arts).

The key competences are all interdependent, and the emphasis in each case is on critical thinking, creativity, initiative, problem solving, risk assessment, decision taking and constructive management of feelings.

The EU key competences comprise a single-dimensional framework, i.e. they do not offer differentiation by level.

KEY COMPETENCES AND EMPLOYABILITY OF POSTGRADUATES IN EUROPE

Chapter 4

Key competences and employability of postgraduates in Europe

This chapter reviews the available data on postgraduate employment and employability in Europe and individual member states. Of particular interest is the perceived mismatch between higher education provision and identified labour market needs particular in the transversal competences associated with 'work readiness' rather than in technical knowledge and abilities.

Furthermore, the percentage of the population qualified to postgraduate level remains broadly stable across Europe despite clear evidence of higher rates of employment and lower growth in unemployment rates for those qualified to Masters level (albeit with significant gender differences).

4.1. Key Competences and socio-economic development in Europe

Many countries emphasize master's degree and doctoral-level attainment to become competitive in what is perceived as a global knowledge economy. Frequently, those with postgraduate qualification have a high level of technical knowledge that allows them to become effective researchers in academia but they also often lack many transversal skills demanded by firms (such as managerial and entrepreneurial skills). As a result, evidence suggest many private enterprises prefer people with bachelor and honours degrees over post graduates as the latter are normally considered less likely to possess business knowledge and commercial instinct[1].

Many **Innovation and Skills Surveys[2]** have pointed out shortages in high-qualified workers in firms. Such skill shortages may inhibit innovation by, for example, less effective new product development processes or creating difficulties for introducing new working practices or technical changes.

1 OECD (2011), Skills for Innovation and Research. ***OECD Innovation Strategy***. OECD, Paris.
2 See for example: Scottish Employers Skills Surveys (2005) and UK Commission on Employment & Skills (2009) ***Ambition 2020: world class skills and jobs for the UK.*** UKCES

INSEAD[3] judged Europe to be under equipped with "global knowledge economy" talent, reducing the capacity to innovate, ability to lead in cross cultural environments, ability to manage teams, and capacity to address new issues (OECD, 2010).

Many studies have demonstrated that companies suffer from **barriers to innovation**, which may be caused by either external or internal factors (financial constraints, international marketing of innovate products, finding suitable partners with knowledge resources, etc.) and are not limited to specific countries in Europe. One of the primary barriers faced by firms, especially SMEs, is **finding qualified, suitable human capital** (Tiwari et al. 2007). At some extent, these difficulties can be related to the lack of applicants with specific knowledge and qualifications, but they also reflect broader concerns about the supply of well-rounded candidates with transversal skills.

The **mismatch between formal education and labour needs** is not a new concern, and it is not limited to any specific nation. As the **Generation Europe Foundation** survey illustrates[4], most universities in Europe give too much emphasis on theoretical knowledge and too little preparation about how to face the real world of work. Apart from the importance of transforming education and developing students´ transversal skills, it is necessary to count with new instruments to measure the skills learnt on the job through labour market experiences and more generally multi-contextual (non formal and informal) learning practices.

4.2. Higher Education Attainment

In 2009, graduation rates for **tertiary-type B programmes (master's degree)** averaged 10% among the 26 OECD countries with comparable data. These programmes are classified at the same level of competence as those more theory-based programmes, but they are often of shorter duration (usually two to three years) and are generally not intended to lead to university-level degrees, but rather to lead directly to the labour market. Some 12% of women received this type of degree, compared to 9% of men.

Within the 21 EU countries of that 26 (EU21), among those countries with a large number of first-time **graduates** from these programmes **Slovenia** (26,5%), **Ireland** (25,6%) and **Spain** (15,3%) had the largest proportion of graduates. In most countries, women have higher graduation rates than men. This difference is specially marked in the case of **Germany** (8,6% men and 19,2% women), **Slovenia** (21,5% men and 31,9% women) and **Czech Republic** (1,9% men and 6,5% women) (see table 1).

Trends in this type of tertiary education vary, even though the OECD average has been stable between 2005 and 2009. Taking into account EU21, the highest **growth** was experienced by **Germany** with an increase of 4% points between 2008 and 2009, followed by **Austria**, with an increase of 2% points for the same period (see table 2).

4.3. Employability

On average across OECD countries, **84% of the population with a tertiary education is in employment**. Overall, employment rates are more than 27% points higher for those with a tertiary education than for those who have not completed an

3 INSEAD (2009), "Who Cares? Who Dares? Providing the Skills for an Innovative and Sustainable Europe", background report prepared for the European Business Summit 2009, www.insead.edu/elab.

4 Generation Europe Foundation (2010) *Employing the Next Generation* GFF.

Figure 1: Tertiary Level (Master Degree) Graduation Rates by Gender in EU21 (2009)

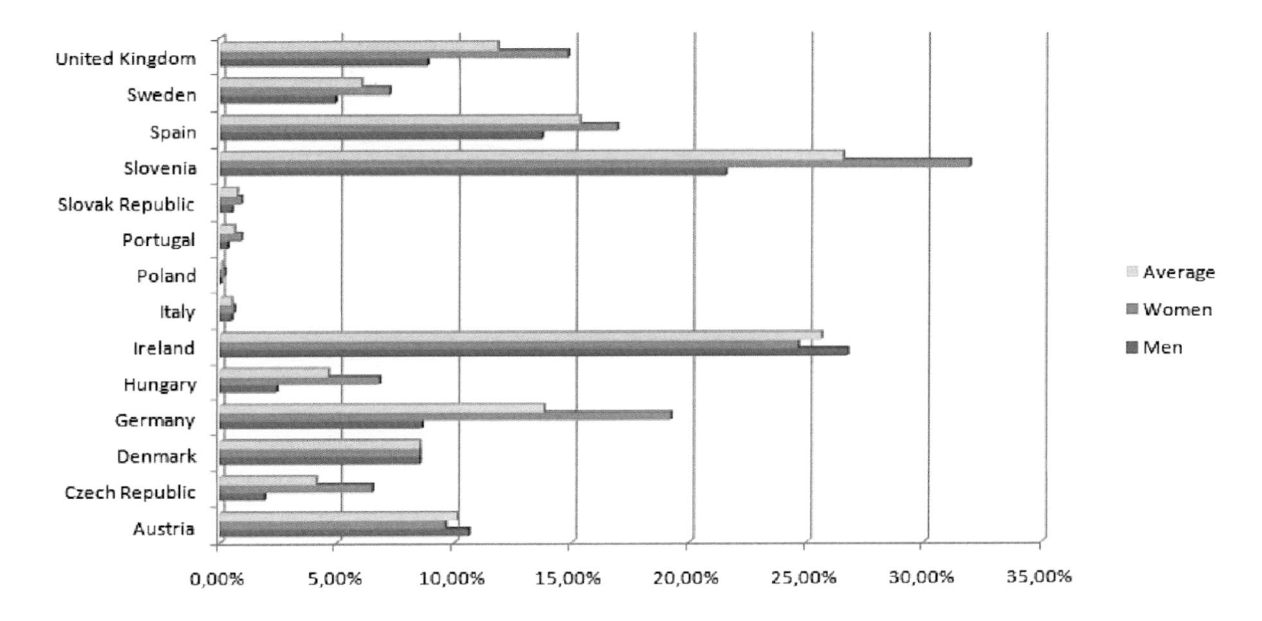

Source: Education at a Glance (OECD, 2011). Missing data for Belgium, Estonia, Finland, France, Greece, Luxemburg and The Netherlands.

Figure 2. Proportion of population qualified to Tertiary Level (Master Degree) in EU21 (2005-2009)

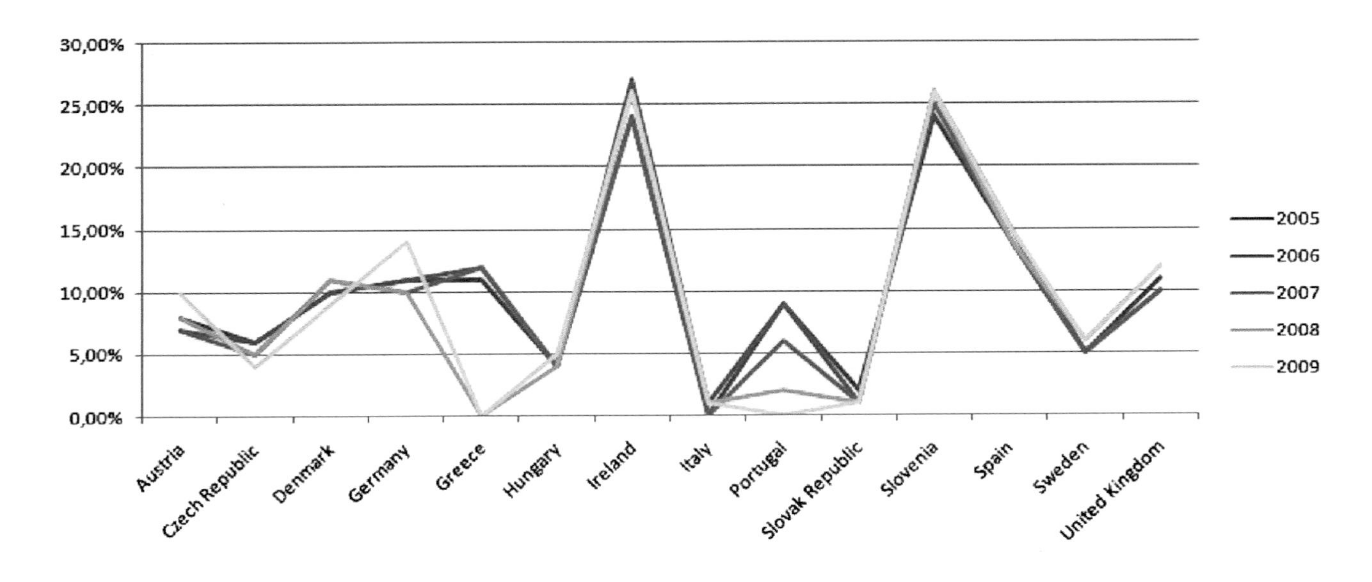

Source: Education at a Glance (OECD, 2011). Missing data for Belgium, Estonia, Finland, France, Luxemburg, The Netherlands and Poland.

Figure 3. Employment Rates for those with Tertiary Level Qualifications by Gender in EU 21 (2009)

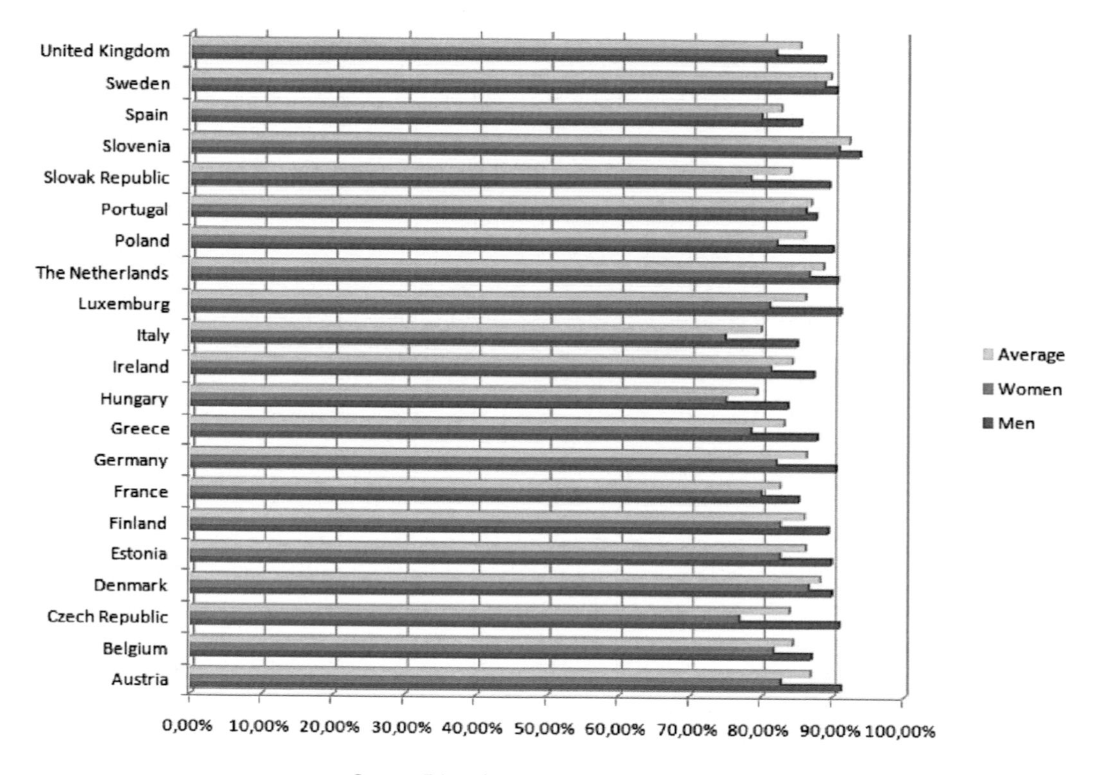

Source: Education at a Glance (OECD, 2011).

Figure 4. Unemployment Rates of those with Tertiary Level Qualifications by Gender in EU 21 (2009)

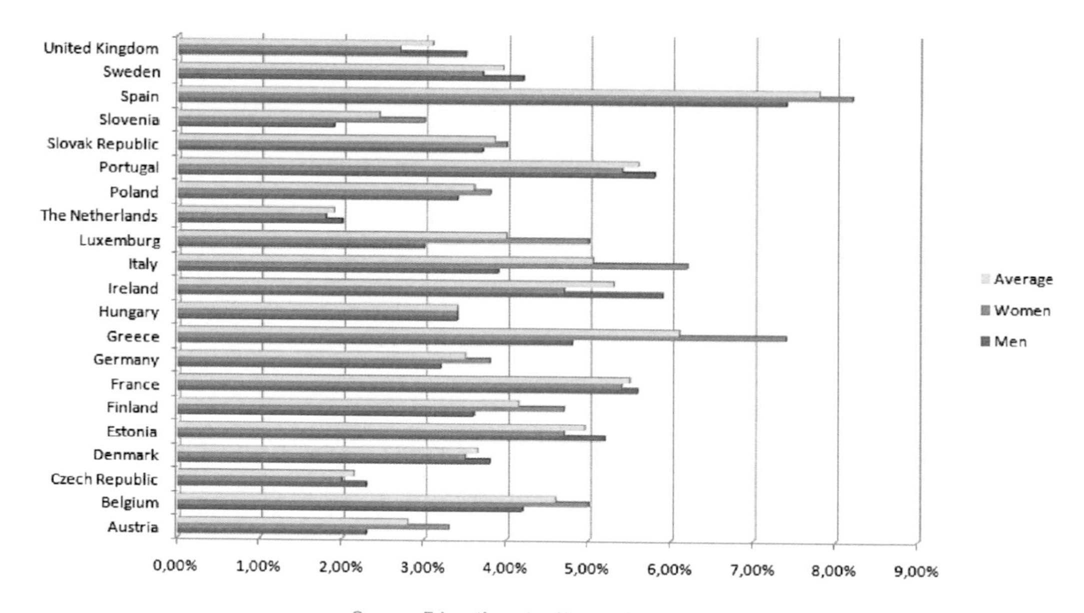

Source: Education at a Glance (OECD, 2011).

upper secondary education (OECD, 2011). On average, **among the most highly qualified adults, men are 9% points more likely than women to be employed**.

However, within the EU21, the **rates of employability** of those with tertiary qualifications vary significantly between countries. Of those with higher levels of employability rates (2009) of this population are **Slovenia** (92,2%), **Sweden** (89,55%) and **Denmark** (88,25%) while those with lower levels include **Hungary** (79,35%) and **Italy** (79,95%). **Czech Republic**, **Slovak Republic** and **Italy** are the countries with higher differences in the ratio of employed highly qualified men and women. In the Czech Republic men are 14% more likely than women to be employed (see table 3).

4.4. Unemployment

In 2009, average **unemployment rate** across OECD countries stood at 4,4% for those with a tertiary education, 6,8% for those with an upper secondary education, and 11,5% for those who have not attained an upper secondary education. Countries with higher unemployment rates for highly qualified people are **Spain** (7,8%), **Greece** (6,1%) and **Portugal** (5,6%). On the contrary, **The Netherlands** (1,9%), **Czech Republic** (2,15%) and **Slovenia** (2,45%) are the countries with lower unemployment rates. The differences by gender are more noticeable in **Greece** and **Italy**, where graduate and postgraduate women are 2% (or higher than 2%) points more likely to be unemployed than men with the same qualification (see table 4).

With few exceptions, **unemployment rates** have increased across OECD countries between 2008 and 2009 but less so for those with higher education qualifications. They increased by 2.8% points for those without an upper secondary education, by 2% points for those with an upper secondary education and by **1.1% points for those with a tertiary education**. The **highest unemployment rate growth** in highly qualified people between 2008 and 2009 was experienced in **Spain** (9.3%) followed by Ireland (6.9%) and finally Greece (6.1%) (see table 5).

This aggregated data points to the increasing problems of increasing unemployment across the EU21 but also to the protection from that trend afforded by Tertiary-Level qualifications. This advantage in the labour market, however, requires continued emphasis on employability in such programmes of study including through transversal Key Competences.

More recent data from Eurostat shows a continuing adverse trend.

Figure 5. Unemployment Rates of Population with Tertiary Level Qualifications in EU21 (2002-2009)

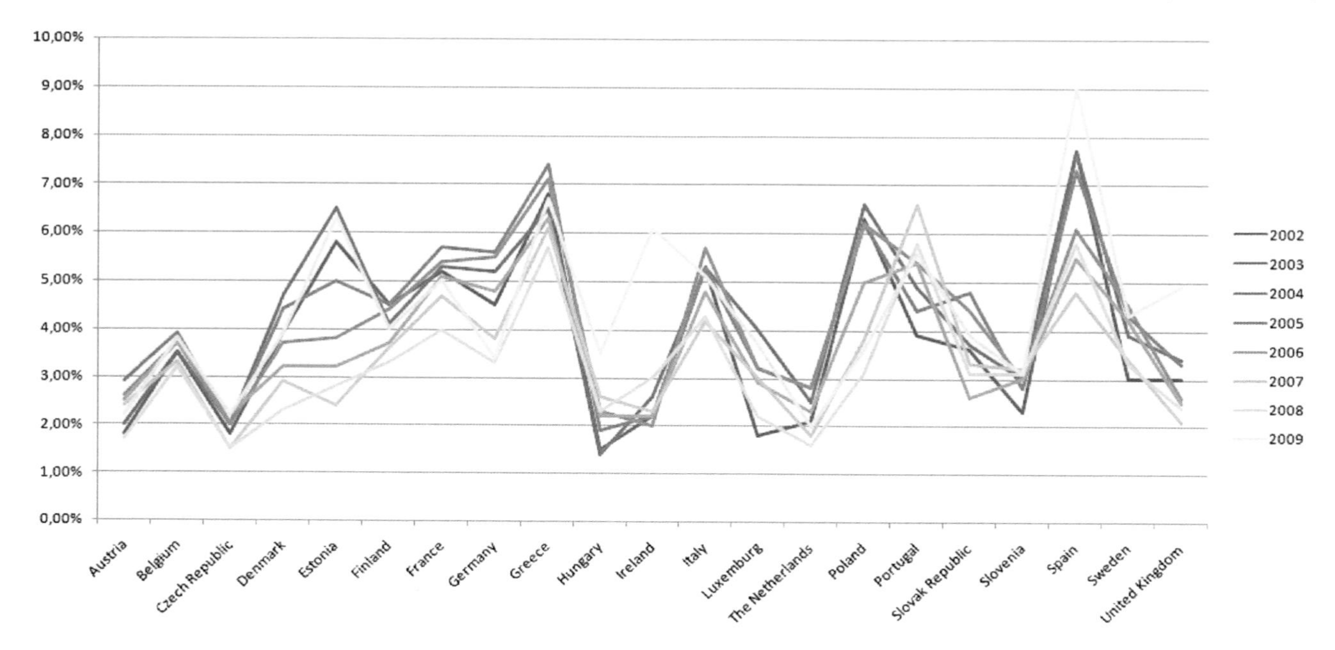

Source: Education at a Glance (OECD, 2011).

Figure 6. Unemployment rates in EU27 (2013)

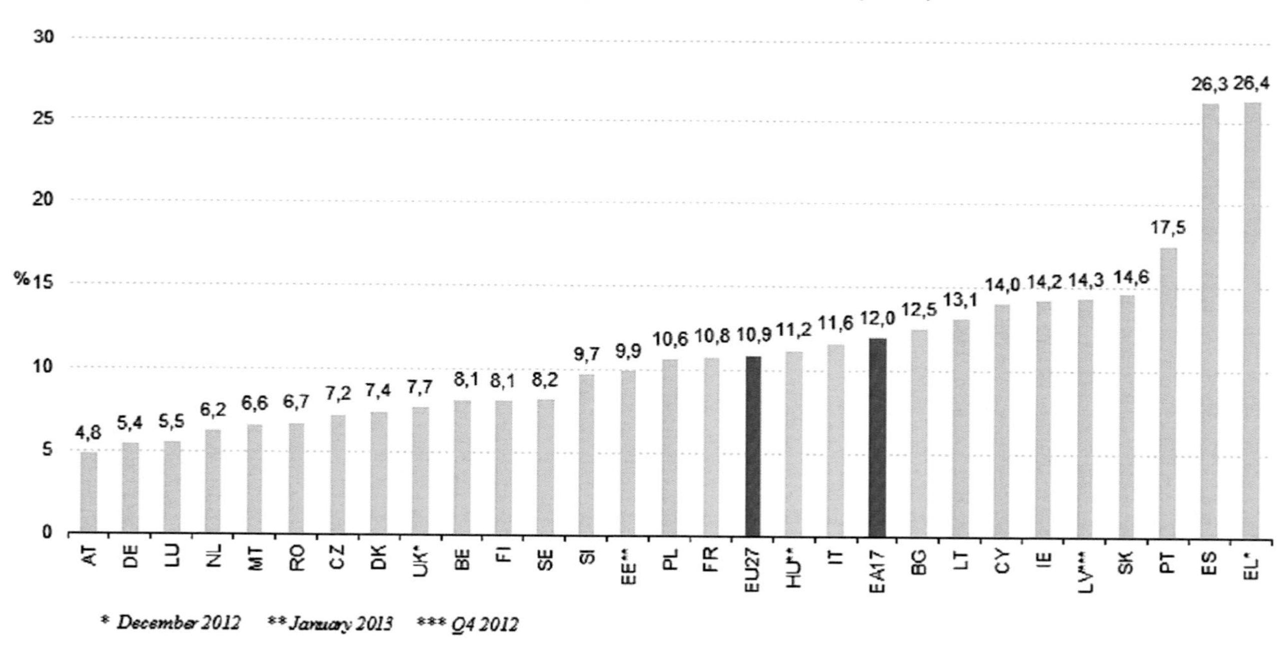

Source: Eurostat EU27 Unemployment rates, seasonally adjusted, Feb 2013.

Figure 7. Youth unemployment rates in EA17 and EU27

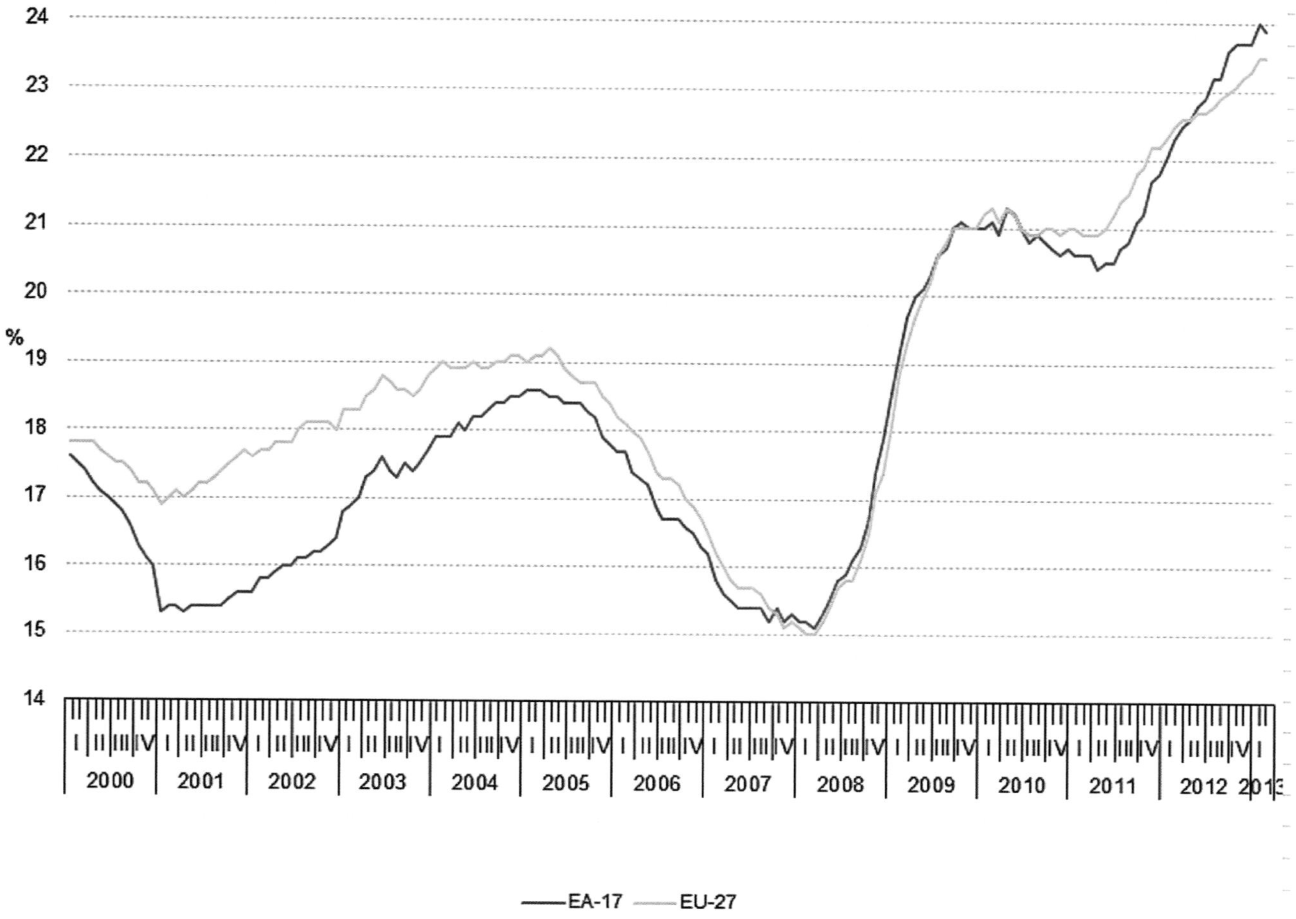

EA-17 EU-27

Source: Eurostat EA17 and EU27 Youth unemployment rates, seasonally adjusted, Feb 2013.

NATIONAL POLICY
CONTEXTS

Chapter 5

National Policy Contexts

This chapter provides an overview of the national policy contexts for those European member states participating in the PROPOUND project: the United Kingdom; Spain; Italy; The Netherlands and Estonia. By overview of national policy contexts, this chapter refers to the national situation with respect to key competences development at higher education level.

5.1. United Kingdom

5.1.1. National Policy

The key aspects of the conceptualisation and implementation of key competences in the UK are summarised here:

Education and Training policy is largely devolved to the administrations in Scotland, Wales and Northern Ireland, with the national government responsible for England. There are many national bodies too such as Sector Skills Councils, professional associations and regulatory bodies. England, Wales and Northern Ireland are very similar, with Scotland having a more distinctive system.

A system of **Functional Skills** and **Key Skills** (**Core Skills** in Scotland) is well established, with formal qualifications readily available. But these are largely aimed at school level education, and entry to Higher Education, apprenticeships or work, and at adult (remedial) education. There is little uniform policy or practice for key competences at bachelor or masters degree levels.

These **Functional/Key/Core Skills** can all be readily mapped onto the eight European Key Competences. But the reverse is not true as the UK system does not (or only barely) covers:

- KC2 Communication in foreign language.
- KC3 (part) Science and technology – although mathematical competence is addressed in the UK key skills.
- KC6 Social and civic.

- KC7 Sense of initiative and entrepreneurship.
- KC8 Cultural awareness and expression.

All UK university degrees, both bachelor and master, have been based on **learning outcomes** for as long as anyone can remember and are described as an "almost universal feature of UK higher education programme" (Quality Assurance Agency, 2007). Furthermore, most degree courses are required to comply with a system of "subject benchmarks" which set out national level requirements for each main subject area. Within that framework, universities have considerable autonomy over their individual programme curricula.

Another significant feature of the UK system is the strong position of the **professional** and in some cases **regulatory bodies**. These organisations accredit individual programmes as providing the knowledge (and often competence) required to practice as a recognised professional, and conduct inspections regularly. Withdrawal of accreditation would in effect often lead to the closure of a programme.

5.1.2. But does it work?

This combination of learning outcomes, subject benchmarks, and professional and/ or regulatory accreditation provides a powerful mechanism whereby key competences (although that term is not used) are embedded within postgraduate programmes. It is common, particularly in vocationally orientated subjects, for such topics to be included and assessed, such as: professional ethics, teamwork, communication, use of ICT, sustainability and environment.

Nevertheless, employers continue to complain about the work readiness of graduates. At a recent London conference on graduate employability, the Chief Executive of the national body for graduate recruiters claimed in his keynote address that graduates cannot talk on a telephone. Employer representatives emphasised that they favour generic over technical skills. Some universities respond that it is not their job to produce "oven-ready" workers.

While such remarks are probably extreme, and perhaps used for theatrical effect, it is clear that there remains dissatisfaction with the employability of new graduates and postgraduates. This view is more strident from the business world, less so from the fields of education, medicine, law.

5.1.3. Current developments

This matter of graduate employability has received significant and sustained media and political attention. The UK Government commissioned a review by Prof. Sir Tim Wilson on business-university collaborations that reported in mid-2012. The Government itself published its own response a few months later, as did other bodies and several individual universities.

A key initiative from the Wilson Review has been the creation of a new national body, under the auspices of the Commission on Employment & Skills, to oversee university-employer engagement at national level.

The Higher Education Achievement Record (HEAR) provides a standardised report of course content in the form of learning outcomes and all a student's achievements at university, including recognised non-academic matters. It therefore provides a mechanism for recording key competences. The Implementation of the HEAR is progressing well, and proving popular with employers and most universities.

The most striking development in the UK (but not in Scotland) has been the recent introduction of very substantial student fees of up to £9,000 per annum for bachelor degrees. The current 2012 student intake has been the first to experience the full effect. It is too early to see what the implications of this will be on postgraduate provision, fees and student numbers, but the cultural effect is already apparent. Students now see themselves as customers of the university, entitled to a good education which they are paying for, and willing to "shop around" to obtain it.

5.2. Spain

5.2.1. National Policy Context

In this section the new **Strategy University 2015**[1] and the specific measures adopted to promote the employability of university students and graduates in Spain is described. The **CertiUni initiative** will be introduced as a 'bottom up' example of the assessment, development and accreditation of key competences in Spanish Universities.

Following the **European Agenda of Modernization of Universities (2006 and 2011),** the Spanish Universities have initiated a process of institutional modernization in the framework of an action defined as **Strategy University 2015**. In this strategy, the concept of **employability** has a prominent presence to face three main challenges:

- The imbalance between employability and employment.
- A perceived over qualification of university students.
- A brain drain from Spain.

1 Ministry of Education (2010) *University 2015: new funding models for Spanish Universities*.

For that, a **National Employability Commission** at higher education level, under the Ministry of Education, was created in 2011 to monitor the implementation of an **Employability Plan**, which includes the following measures:

- Design new graduate and postgraduate titles using parameters of labour market entry.
- **Creation of Professional Guidance Programmes based on acquisition of transversal competences in Universities.**
- Promotion of the Employability Forum with the Universities´ Social Council and socio-economic agents.
- Implementation of programs of professional initiation for new graduates.
- Creation of a support programme for unemployed university graduates.
- Promotion of entrepreneurship and the creation of new enterprises from university research.
- Participation of professionals and employers in university activities.
- Creation of specific calls for proposals related to the promotion of the employability of university graduates.
- Creation of the University Student Council of the State to promote the participation of the students in university policy decisions.

The specific measures are directed to supply the right mix of skills and competences for the labour market: employability and entrepreneurship. It is a priority within this strategy that *"Universities provide the appropriate capacities and competences for the labour market. The employability of university graduates must be enhanced and the entrepreneurial training and culture of students and researchers should be encouraged".*

In this new context, traditional paradigms of assessment, teaching and learning in Spanish Higher Education are undergoing a transformation with the implementation of the European Higher Education Area. One of the basic milestones of this model is the design of a competence-based curriculum, that is, a set of skills developed by the student after having direct interaction with certain knowledge and practice.

Competence based education has many challenges and difficulties for teachers, especially in Spain, where appropriate experience and training to tackle this new education model is still lacking. The first explicit references to competences appear in **Organic Law on Education** in 2006[2]. The **Spanish Higher Education Qualification Framework** (MECES), inspired by the "Dublin Descriptors" has been established by the **Royal Decree 1027/2011 of July 15**, setting the basis for a four level structure to profile a person depending on the acquired knowledge and certification for each stage of the HE system (Bachelors´, Masters´ and Doctorate). Also, specific transversal competences are described in the White Papers of each Faculty of Spanish Universities as necessary for obtaining different degrees.

Recently, some **bottom up initiatives** from more innovative Spanish universities have appeared. In 2009, a group of ten public and private HEIs, led by the Confederation of Rectors of Spanish Universities (CRUE), has launched a **virtual platform for the assessment and certification of the key competences acquired by undergraduate and postgraduate students: CertiUni (University Certification Platform).** The system has a voluntary character and is based on an open call in the ten Universities participating in the initiative. CertiUni is based on five main groups of competences:

2 Ley Orgánica 2/2006, de 3 de mayo, de Educación.

- Personal competences.
- Management competences.
- Learning potential.
- Participate and relational competences.
- Entrepreneurship competences.

The assessment is developed in the Universities´ faculties and centres and is based on test techniques through web technologies. The types of exercises included are tasks of work, situation tests, tasks execution tests and potential tests. External public agencies and private companies are responsible to carry out the assessment and to accredit the acquired competences.

5.3. Italy

5.3.1. National policy

In the Italian school system the concept of competence started to be considered in 2000 (Berlinguer-De Mauro Reform) becoming codified since August 2007[3]with national recommendations for primary school and compulsory education up to the age of 16.

Only with the new National Recommendations in September 2012[4], the European Key Competence Framework is mentioned as the target for education. This target is to be reached in primary and secondary schools and beyond, coherently with continuous education and lifelong learning.

These Recommendations adopt the European eight Key Competences at the primary and secondary school level, adapted and translated to the national school system curricula. In accordance

3 (D.M. n. 139 del 22 agosto 2007).
4 Indicazioni Nazionali 2012.

with the European Qualifications Framework, they are the general (compulsory) reference set of learning outcomes for teachers to design, deliver assess and evaluate programmes of learning.

The overall formative and summative assessment will be the teachers' responsibility. However, the National Institution for Evaluation (L'Istiuto Nazionale di Valutazione – INVALSI) has to assess the target learning outcomes included in the National Recommendations, discouraging a culture of test-based evaluation.

At the end of primary and secondary school, students' target competences will be recognised, assessed and certified in accordance with school autonomy, through methods and tools established at national level[5].

However, the current policy framework for the adoption of Key Competences does not extend to higher education.

In Italy, following the Bologna Process, higher education was reorganised into three levels, the bachelor (two years); the master (two years + 3 years) and the PhD (3 years). The Bachelor, Master and PhD Degrees correspond to the EQF levels 6, 7 and 8. However, no National Qualification Framework has been developed based on the EQF or the eight European Key Competences. The reform of higher education with the Law 204 elaborated in 2010 and put into action at the end of January 2011, is mainly focused on organisation, recruitment of academic staff, efficiency and internationalisation. The internationalisation of Italian universities is a crucial point in the latest reform and this issue can become the entry point for drawing attention to competences and the EQF in higher education.

5 Italian Law nr 92 of 28 June 2012 and the related decree of 11 January 2011.

5.3.2. Focus on access and transition

In June 2012, ISFOL, the national research body related to the Ministry of Labour providing technical and scientific support to the central Government and the regional and local institutions, issued the first Italian report on national qualifications cross-referenced to the EQF[6]. This is the first attempt at referencing national education qualifications to the EQF. Following public consultations, the report is currently being revised and adjusted. Accordingly, the topic of national reference frameworks for education and above all higher education is only now moving to consideration of issues of implementation.

However, it can be stated that postgraduate programmes correspond to the EQF level 7[7]. Under this framework, in the ISFOL first reference activity, the expected learning outcomes are as follows in Table 8:

Table 8. Excerpt from ISFOL June 2012 on the Learning Outcome Framework proposed for Postgraduate programmes, EQF Level 7 (in progress).

Postgraduate degrees can be issued to students who:	
Italian	English
Abbiano dimostrato conoscenze e capacità di compresione che estendono e/o rafforzano quelle tipicamente associate al primo ciclo e consentono di elaborare e/o applicare idee originali, spesso in un contesto di ricerca;	Have demonstrated enhancement or enrichment of knowledge and understanding developed in the previous cycle, enabling students to elaborate and apply new and origianl ideas in research contexts mainly;

6 Isfol, giugno 2012.
7 See Bologna process, http://ec.europa.eu/education/higher-education/bologna_en.htm

Siano capaci di applicare le loro conoscenze, capacità di comprensione e abilità nel risolvere problemi a tematiche nuove o non familiari, inserite in contesti più ampi (o interdisciplinari) connesi al proprio settore di studio;	Are able to aply their knowledge and understanding to solving new and unfamiliar problems within broader or interdisciplinary contexts related to their sector of study;
Abbiano la capacità di integrare le conoscenze e gestire la complessità, nonché di formulare giudizi sulla base di informazioni limitate o incomplete, includendo la riflessione sulle responsabilità sociali ed etiche collegate all'applicazione delle loro conoscenze e giudizi;	Are able to integrate their knowledge and manage complexity, formulate judgments on the basis of limited or uncompleted information including reflections on ethics and social responsibility related to the application of their knowledge;
Sappiaro comunicare in modo chiaro e privo di ambiguità le loro conclusioni, nonché le conoscenze e la ratio ad esse sottese, a interlocutori specialisti e non specialisti;	Are able to communicate their thoughts and conclusions clearly, as well as their knowledge and reasons behind, to specialists and also not expert people;
Abbiano sviluppato quelle capacità di apprendimento che consentano loro di continuare a studiare per lo più in modo autodiretto o autonomo.	Have developed learning abilities enabling them to go on studying autonomously.

Source: Excerpt from ISFOL, *Primo Rapporto Italiano Di Referenziazione Delle Qualificazioni Al Quadro Europeo EQF*, giugno 2012, in progress, under consultation.

Interestingly the emerging Key Competences are Communication (1,2), Learning to Learn (5), Civic competence (6).

Concerning Key Competences as a whole, thanks to the National Recommendations (2007, 2012), experimentation has been carried on at secondary level, both technical-professional and high school, to recognise and assess Key Competences and to improve them. Yet, such experiments are still missing in higher education. If career services in Italy are implementing training measures on "soft skills", the related diplomas are not compulsory in the university programmes and do not provide credits.

5.4. The Netherlands

5.4.1. Dutch policy for curricular reform in higher education

The main objective of the Dutch strategy for Validation of Prior Learning (VPL) is to create a lifelong learning attitude in which updating and upgrading someone's competences is at the heart of learning strategies. Curricular reform in HE therefore focuses on the assessment of the competences that are collected in a portfolio with the goal of getting exemptions or a diploma, referring to a specific standard. The portfolio is in this context mainly a showcase of only the competences that matter for the standard itself; all the other personal competences are irrelevant. The choice for a specific standard is in practice more steered by the availability of an actual standard than by a free personal choice. This is because most of the times a school - as the keeper of the standard(s) – tends to look more to the best chance of success when measured against any given standard than to the best match of a standard and personal ambitions. So, in effect, VPL is more standard-steered, and as most standards are kept by schools (upper secondary and higher vocational levels) also strongly school-steered.

5.4.2. Focus on access and transition

When focusing on the way that the concept of key competences for lifelong learning is embedded in a national learning culture, it is of particular interest to investigate how the models and procedures of crediting learning outcomes are targeting two "interfaces" of the countries´ qualification systems: "access" into the qualification system and "transition" within the qualification system and between qualification subsystems.

Access refers to conditions, circumstances or

requirements governing admittance to and participation in initial training (e.g. from vocational preparation into initial training).

Transition describes the move within the qualification system (e.g. within "vocation families" (integration of former "drop outs"), from school based training into dual training) and / or from one qualification subsystem into another (e.g. from initial training to further qualification, from initial training to academic training). At both interfaces challenges and framework conditions for credit transfer might differ from country to country.

Formal entrance and access are organised for bachelor-programmes in different procedures for different target-groups:

- For **young people**: the minimum admission requirement is either a secondary school diploma (HAVO or VWO) or a level-4 vocational diploma. For admission to higher education, pupils are required to have completed at least one of the subject clusters that fulfils the requirements for the higher education programme in question. A quota (*numerus fixus*) applies to admission to certain programmes, primarily in the medical sciences, and places are allocated using a weighted lottery.
- For admission to **master's programmes**, a bachelor's degree in one or more specified disciplines is required, in some cases in combination with other requirements. Graduates with an HBO bachelor's may have to complete additional requirements for admission to a WO master's programme.
- For **adult learners** the same applies as above: normally a still valid, formal diploma is the ticket to entry to higher education. Alternative routes for access are: (i) a so-called 21+ test in which the adult is tested on the levels in Dutch, English, mathematics and social-cultural knowledge; (ii) international diploma recognition; and (iii) a VPL-procedure.

The general question is: does the debate on key competences have an influence on existing procedures for access to and/or accrediting of learning outcomes in the Netherlands?

In general the answer to this question for the Netherlands is no. As is known, each EU-member state has to link its National Qualifications Framework to the European Qualifications Framework. Apart from this priority on implementing the learning outcomes-approach as propagated by the EQF initiative, there is an issue in the Netherlands on the question how to activate Accreditation of Prior Learning (APL) as an effective instrument for facilitating lifelong learning that appeals to the citizen and other stakeholders.

The above question emphasises the need to broaden access to higher education and includes also the necessity of strengthening the transferability of competences between organisations on the basis of a learning outcomes approach. The acceptance of models for the recognition of key competences is one of the main features of such a desired, dynamic education and training system. The route of applying concepts of Key Competences has to and will be taken (and strengthened) in the coming years. Both VPL-methodology as well as the concept of Key Competences help in strengthening the accessibility and transitional usage of learning outcomes.

5.5. Estonia

Here, the specific measures adopted to promote the employability of university students and graduates in Estonia through the Estonian Qualifications

Authority is described. The Estonian Qualifications Framework (EstQF) has **eight levels**[8]. The descriptions of the qualification levels are identical with the EQF level descriptions. EstQF is a comprehensive framework[9] consisting of four sub-frameworks for:

- General education qualifications.
- Vocational education and training (VET) qualifications.
- Higher education qualifications.
- Occupational (work based sectoral) qualifications.

Level descriptions of sub-frameworks are defined in the corresponding national educational standards:

- National Curriculum for Basic Schools.
- Simplified National Curriculum for Basic Schools.
- National Curriculum for Upper Secondary Schools.
- Standard of VET.
- Standard of Higher Education.

There are two types of competences in general education: general competences and field specific competences. General competences and field specific competences together cover all EU Key Competences for Lifelong Learning.

The LOs of higher education qualifications have been defined in the Standard of Higher Education[10] as:

8 See http://www.kutsekoda.ee/fwk/contenthelper/10445708/10445709
9 See http://kutsekoda.ee/fwk/contenthelper/10447220/10447221
10 See https://www.riigiteataja.ee/akt/13099603

The knowledge, skills and attitudes acquired as a result of studies which are described at the minimum level which is necessary for the completion of a programme, module or subject.

Descriptions of generic LOs for the four types of higher education qualifications are compatible with Dublin descriptors but do not copy them. No attempt has been made to differentiate between professional and transferable LOs. Particularly, in order to be awarded a ***magistrikraad*** (Master's degree), a student shall:

- Have systematic overview and broad knowledge of concepts, theories and research methods of the field of study.
- Know the theoretical development trends, current problems and potential applications in the field of study.
- Have in depth-knowledge in a narrower research field of the field of research.
- Be able to identify and create interdisciplinary connections.
- Be able to independently and creatively identify and formulate problems and /or research questions related to the field of study and be able to solve them with appropriate measures within given timeframes and within limited information, using of knowledge of other fields as necessary.
- Be able to select and use appropriate methods and technologies when solving problems of the field of study, and to model and/or assess the potential results.
- Be able to critically evaluate his or her activities when solving problems and/or research questions of the field of study.
- Be prepared to work in an area of activity requiring professional qualifications, showing

initiative, responsibility, leadership and team work skills.

- Be able to hand down with competence his or her knowledge by teaching, instruction or in another manner.
- Be able to present and reason orally or in written form in the language of instruction and a foreign language essential for his or her field of study the problems relating to the field of study, conclusions and the underlying theories, and to participate in relevant discussions of both corresponding specialists and non-specialists.
- Be willing to actively participate in the civil society and demonstrate tolerance towards diversity of attitudes and values.
- Be able to act ethically in complex situations, be aware of the ethical aspects, possibilities, restrictions and social role of his or her activities and be able to provide reasoned assessment in issues concerning his or her field of study;
- be able to evaluate his or her need, and the need of others, of continuing education and professional development, and have command of effective methods necessary for independent study.
- Be able to continue studies or participate in research, act as a specialist or developer in his or her field, including internationally.

All types of qualifications in Estonia contain LOs referring to key competences. As a rule, these are assessed indirectly in the process of subject or module assessment (general education, VET, higher education qualifications) or in the process of occupational competences assessment (occupational qualifications).

THE PROPOUND PROJECT

Chapter 6

The PROPOUND Project

The main objective *of the PROPOUND project is to propel the modernization agenda of Universities, promoting curricular reforms directed to improve the employability of Postgraduate students.* The PROPOUND project seeks to develop a Key Competences Model for University Postgraduate Programmes. Key competences refer to those non-disciplinary - or transversal – competences, additional to subject specific content of a particular postgraduate programme, that are critical to employability and employment skills. The project aims to encourage dialogue and cooperation between universities and employers on the design of innovative curricular strategies and tools in university postgraduate programmes that respond to labour market needs and promote the development, assessment and certification of key competences of graduates benefiting from these programmes.

This chapter provides a summary of the findings of the PROPOUND project research and development activities.

6.1. Recognition of Key Competences

As defined in the Cedefop Glossary[1], Key Competences are "needed to live in a contemporary knowledge society", and they are increasingly requested at work. The Commission underlines that Key Competences can be regarded as sets of *learning outcomes*; hence, they can be *learned* and *developed* by everyone. Generally speaking, disciplines (e.g. sciences) produce specialist knowledge and in some cases even ***specialist competences***. On the contrary, when speaking about ***key competences*** we refer to the so-called ***competences for life***. Key competences are not specific to a given discipline. They are cross-cutting or transversal to any discipline. Hence everybody should acquire such abilities as we are dealing with ***competences for life***. It is a common view in the traditional education systems that the development of key competences is left or delegated to the student´s own talent and knack, depending mainly on self-capabilities and aptitudes. In fact, in a traditional view of education, what is taught and

1 Cedefop (2011) Glossary, ***Quality in Education and Training***, Publications Office of the European Union.

learned at school is usually much more related with ***subjects to be read in the text-books (i.e. knowledge)***, rather than ***skills to be experienced (i.e. competence)***. Hence, key competences cannot be taught with traditional methods and do not belong to any specific classical disciplines, either. Coherently, it is not common to recognise them formally in education programmes. Yet, key competences are continuously developed informally[2], at any learning level, not only in daily life but just even at school as ***unintentional by-products*** within formal courses. Such richness is likely to get lost if we are not able to detect value and recognise it.

With respect to this, key competences development is to become conscious and fostered intentionally[3]through proper didactic approaches. That not only is true for *key* competences but anytime we refer to ***competences*** versus knowledge. "Competences" are the "proven ability ***to use*** knowledge, skills and personal, social and/or methodological abilities [...]"[4 5]. "Competences" draw on dynamic concepts and ***holistic processes***; they are concerned with know-how and understanding, with behaviours and performance. Therefore, competences and key competences all the more can be developed and enhanced by effective didactic methods based on action and reflection[6] and encouraging personal engagement, being proactive and enterprising[7]and complementing lessons in the classroom.

Hence, we can reasonably say that key competences, as unintended by-products of activities including formal education, can be translated into intentional and explicit learning processes to be managed and "controlled" by students with the support of teaching staff and proper didactic methods. Coherently, we can therefore include them in university programmes. On the methodological side, what we need for formal recognition is just to make key competences explicit in a reference LOs-based framework, define the related assessment criteria, and identify the proper situations enhancing them, including didactic methods. Consensus building within university staff and students' communities is of course essential for formal recognition, too. The "Learning Outcome"-based model from the EQF[8] is the basis for integrating key competences to university programmes and formal recognition. Using LOs allows going beyond the classical disciplinary content (namely the traditional knowledge) and including dynamic elements. At the same time, LOs suggest the way of recognising the learning content, namely how to assess them, deal with them, make them concrete.

Moreover, ***competence*** as the "proven ability to use ***knowledge, skills and personal, social and/or methodological abilities in work or study situations and in professional and personal development***" [9 10] tells us at least two things: any competences are a complex mix of different dimensions, namely knowledge, skills and attitudes; they are recognised when the ability to use them in specific situations is demonstrated. Hence, there is a competence only when there is a ***full observable behaviour*** integrating knowledge, skills and attitudes; furthermore, as it is

2 Cedefop (2009) ***European Guidelines for validating non-formal and informal learning***, Publications Office of the European Communities.

3 Cedefop (2009) ***European Guidelines for validating non-formal and informal learning***, Publications Office of the European Communities.

4 European Qualifications Framework for Lifelong Learning (EQF) http://ec.europa.eu/dgs/education_culture/publ/pdf/eqf/broch_en.pdf

5 Cedefop (2011) Glossary, ***Quality in Education and Training***, Publications Office of the European Union.

6 Kolb, D.A. (1984) ***Experiential Learning***, Englewood Cliffs, NJ, Prentice Hall.

7 Zimmerman, B.J. (2000) ***Self-regulatory cycles of learning***. In: Straka, G.A., Conceptions of Self-Directed Learning: Theoretical and Conceptual Considerations, New York: Waxmann, pp.221-34

8 European Qualifications Framework for Lifelong Learning (EQF) http://ec.europa.eu/dgs/education_culture/publ/pdf/eqf/broch_en.pdf

9 European Qualifications Framework for Lifelong Learning (EQF) http://ec.europa.eu/dgs/education_culture/publ/pdf/eqf/broch_en.pdf

10 Cedefop (2011) Glossary, Quality in Education and Training, Publications Office of the European Union.

an ***observable behaviour***, it necessarily shows and acts in a specific context. If such mixture of dimensions is not translated in any context, there is not a real behaviour and not any competences either. Accordingly, someone can exert a competence in a situation but may need to take some time to transfer or translate that competence into another situation. Competences are not ***context-free***, rather, they are ***context specific***[11], and that is, competences are ***situated***. This is very important for formal recognition and the related assessment methods as well as didactic methods once again.

It is feasible and expected to reach formal recognition of key competences. However, it will not be possible unless learning outcomes and competence based approaches effectively become the foundation of a new paradigm. Moreover, the context, whether work or study situations, does play a role. It should not be underestimated; rather, it is to be valued when developing competences either in general or specific.

Finally, the eight key competences, and in particular ***learning to learn***, can be considered as competences "enabling" disciplinary learning and further competences. That is another aspect to be taken into account in deciding which and how key competences are to be included in programmes for formal recognition.

6.1.1. Two possible routes for key competences formal recognition

The purpose of PROPOUND is to help the higher education system take a step forward in the actions aimed at including key competences in postgraduate programmes and recognising them formally. We discuss two examples expressing two possible solutions to the issue referred to as Route A (Discrete) and Route B (Embedded).

Route A Discrete: "developing key competences aside" – is taken from the Pilot Action conducted by the Fundación General Universidad de Granada Empresa (FGUGREM) and Scienter CID (Propound, 2012): the key competences are developed outside the master / postgraduate programmes, as specific learning units of a dedicated course. In this case, certification will specifically be referred to the key competences assessed after completing the related learning units. This is an example of key competences "developed" through a dedicated set of activities that is reported and a training course that is discussed. In the pilot intervention, the target group involved was formed by six students of the Master in "3D Animation of Characters" of the University of Granada. The skills selected for enhancement were about Communication. Such skills are mainly related to Key Competences 6, ***Social and Civic,*** and 7, ***Sense of initiative***. The chosen approach to select the key competences to be enhanced was based on the Personal Development Planning Method (PDP). Such method supports a "learner to reflect upon their own learning, performance and/or achievement and to plan for their personal, educational and career development. [....] Effective PDP improves the capacity of individuals to review, plan and take responsibility for their own learning and to understand what and how they learn"[12]. Accordingly, the PDP approach itself contributes towards the enhancement of key competences and in particular ***learning to learn*** key competence. In accordance with the PDP method, the ***side*** key competence programme included three phases:

1. Self-assessment of key competences by students (based on the PDP principles).

11 Bojatzis, R.E. (1982) The competent manager: A model for effective performance, John Wiley & Sons.

12 QAA (2009) Personal development planning: guidance for institutional policy and practice in higher education, The Quality Assurance Agency for Higher Education.

2. A training course on the missing key competences.
3. External assessment.

Accordingly, a webinar on that topic was delivered, followed by mentoring during the students' internship, with a final self-assessment report. No certification but a statement of attendance was issued.

Route A shows the opportunity to include ***side programmes*** for the development of key competences in university curricula. Even though not compulsory, such programmes can provide credits for the completion of the courses. Very interesting is the use of the PDP and the self-assessment approach to help students become aware of their competences and competence needs; make their skills explicit; showing them actively the way to personal and professional growth. Moreover, under this scenario, internship can be valued and better finalised. In fact, practice is the most suitable way to develop competences; an assessment at the end of internship, even allowing certifications, would enrich this stage. However, in order to get formal recognition, quality-based approaches are needed: how long do such courses have to last? Which qualifications do the teachers have to have? What key competence models are to be transferred? Which kinds of assessment are to be set up? Furthermore, who will pay? These are just some examples of possible aspects to be discussed, shared and agreed by the university communities.

Route B Embedded: "Embedding key competences" from the "Programme Specification for MSc in the Management of Training & Development" (University of Edinburgh 2011): The key competences are developed within existing postgraduate programmes. They are embedded into the set of learning outcomes already defined for master/postgraduate programmes, as integral parts of them. In this case, the final certification refers to the programme as a whole – full qualification. The key competences will be assessed together with the other knowledge, skills and competences, as part of the entire set of learning outcomes to be fulfilled to get the full qualification. An example is reported of key competences developed within existing postgraduate programmes. The example comes from a Master Course in "the Management of Training & Development". In the programme specifications (August 2011), four "Graduate Attributes" (Research and Enquiry; Personal and Intellectual Autonomy; Communication; Personal Effectiveness) have been defined in terms of learning outcomes, context, teaching and assessment settings. Together with the "knowledge and understanding" specifications, they form the programme outcomes.

It is to be highlighted that embedding the key competence development in the master course itself implies a consistent learning outcome-based approach. Key Competences translated into learning outcomes are to be included in the overall set of learning outcomes of any reference university courses. In the University of Edinburgh's example, most key competences form the overall set of the programme outcomes, together with the reference discipline knowledge and understanding (namely "training"). To get the related degrees, students must demonstrate the whole set of learning outcomes, which include key competences. Hence, key competences are formally recognized directly in the courses. Learning Outcomes are the basis; didactic approaches are also a strategic factor to enhance key competences as well as assessment criteria. If all these components are coherently built-in, the richness of learning processes is kept, valued and recognized. In this way, the key competences acquisition looks "true" and "real" because it is not separated from the experiential streams, but "embedded" ***in work or study situation.*** Transparency and transferability are guaranteed once again by learning outcomes and the explicit descriptions of learning sets.

6.1.2. Conclusion

The possible advantage in adopting Route A is to be found in standardisation and transferability. Being generic and cross-cutting, any university programme in the future can include the key-competence diploma or certification obtained through the completion of the key competence course. On the other hand, Route B solves the standardisation issue with the reference key competence framework shared and agreed by university communities. The advantages of Route B are clear. Route B is able to turn the unwitting, by-product key competences into explicit and conscious outcomes. Route B is able to surface the hidden richness, value and exploit it, as well as enhancing it with focused and improving actions. It accepts key competences to be developed by action, coming out of the students' learning practice instead of teaching lessons, and the teaching staff to be mainly a supporter, a coach. This view fulfils the other competence requirement, being a *holistic process*, a *complex mixture* of dimensions.

Both routes to formal recognition of key competences can be fostered, taking into account their mutual criticalities, limits and opportunities. The specific university contexts will play a relevant role in influencing the choices for one or another approach. On the whole, one of the key success factors for including key competences in the formal recognition process is *consensus* within the university communities of teaching staff and students as well. Hence, the first step is deciding together that key competences are to be formally recognised. From a methodological point of view, the main steps include:

- Describing key competences in terms of learning outcomes; adopting a common and shared reference framework. (In this respect, national frameworks should be available for customizations in each specific contexts; it is also possible to use frameworks already developed and agreed at European level).
- Defining the related assessment criteria.
- Identifying and making explicit which learning outcomes of the reference framework can be achieved in Masters Courses (even unintentionally) and assessed.
- Considering what should be improved and how (e.g. just with didactic methods or with specific *ad hoc* courses) to get formal recognition of the whole set of key competences learning outcomes.

6.2. Assessment Methodologies for Key Competences

The following section provides an overview of the current approaches to the assessment of key competences at higher education level in Europe. This includes: the context, functions and uses assigned to assessment; current trends in the assessment of key competences; the main challenges in the assessment of key competences; preconditions in the assessment of key competences at higher education level. The main conclusion is presented, focusing on the need to design comprehensive strategies for the introduction of the assessment of key competences at university level in Europe. Particular strategies for assessment are then presented in the PROPOUND Action Plan.

6.2.1. Concept of Assessment of Key Competences

According to the European Commission[13], assessment should be learner-centred, that is, it should give valuable and forward-looking information for the individual and can be defined as "the process in which information is collected about competences developed by an individual and they are compared with the profile of the competences required by a job". As with all forms of assessment, the assessment of competences should be fair, reliable and valid. In addition, equity is related to the social nature of assessment and highlights the need to consider differences that are not the focus of an assessment but could influence it.

6.2.2. Current issues in the assessment of key competences

Current issues in the practices of the **assessment** of key competences include:

- Curricula changes not being reflected in changes in assessment practices.
- A tendency by the academic community, education managers and policy makers to focus on technical and subject domain-specific competences rather than on transversal key competences.

Given the widespread recognition that assessment strongly influences teaching and learning, it is clear that current issues in the assessment of key competences militates against the development of transversal key competences in learners.

13 European Commission Staff Working Document 371 (2012), Assessment of Key Competences in initial education and training: policy guidance.

6.2.3. Challenges in the assessment of key competences

Key competences: *manifest themselves in action and behaviour in certain contexts, we have to infer them indirectly to the underlying competences and connected attributes. At the same time, competences cannot be displayed or detected by single, isolated performances, since they are supposed to prove themselves cross-contextually* (Barth 2009). So, the individual acquires transferable competences when s/he is able to combine and apply knowledge, abilities and skills to face new problems and unforeseen situations. Hence:

- Methodologies of assessment have to be specific to capture the added value of learning (knowledge, skills and competences) that occurs outside formal contexts.
- Assessment procedures of transversal competences should include a combination of approaches and methods as no method alone provides a complete overview of key competences acquired by an individual.

6.2.4. Preconditions for the assessment of key competences: the articulation of learning outcomes

Learning Outcomes are statements of what a learner should be able to do or be and contrast with learning inputs such as time, location and method (CEDEFOP, 2008). However, although the importance of key competences is widely recognized, they are generally not specified in learning outcomes, and this conclusion is **especially visible at higher education level**.

The pilot actions developed by PROPOUND provide specific examples on how some key competences (such as *learn to learn*) have been made "assessment-ready" by specifying them as concrete learning outcomes. The conclusions achieved can be helpful to clarify the different options available for describing levels or stages of learners´ progress and to indicate in what contexts and for what purposes these are most useful.

6.2.5. Overview of valuable examples in assessment of key competences at University level

This section aims to provide an overview of the current trends in the assessment of key competences at University level based on the valuable examples collected in the institutions of the consortium partners (Universities and Foundations) as well as in the pilot actions developed in the framework of PROPOUND project. This section of the report presents practical examples of summative assessments using: (a) standardised tests; (b) attitudinal questionnaires; and (c) performance based assessment.

Standardized tests

Standardized tests can contribute to the assessment of key competences as far they include items with "*structure and content that reproduce real life contexts authentically; multiple steps requiring a chain of reasoning and a range of competences and a range of formats allowing responses that require different competences*"[8]. Most of the standardized tests used at university level are focused on key competences associated with technical and discipline-specific subjects.

As discussed above, the CertiUni Project in Spain aims to address this by developing a virtual platform for the assessment and certification of key competences of undergraduate and postgraduate students.

CertiUni Project: University Certification Platform

Launched in 2009, CertiUni is a shared Evaluation and Accreditation System of the Spanish Universities for the assessment of the transversal competences most demanded in the Education Area.

The assessments developed have both summative and formative functions. The Key Competences Framework of Reference is called Participative and Personal Competences (PPC) and Extended PPC. The assessments of Key Competences are based en test techniques through web technologies using:

Tasks of Work: the assessed candidate must manage his/her time and actions to achieve an final objetive.

Situation Tests: based on critical incidents where the assessed candidates must take decisions.

Tasks Execution Tests: to identify the most significant behaviour trends of the assessed candidates.

Potential Tests: tests of maximun performance to assess mental and cognitive aptitudes.

The CertiUni assessments support an online programme of key competence development within components on: team work; communication; leadership; customer orientation; negotiation; self-management, and achievement of results.

Attitudinal questionnaires

Attitudinal questionnaires have some limited benefits in assessing key competences and should be used with other techniques. The Fondazione Politecnico di Milano has created an Observatory for the identification and assessment of the key competences to be included in the Engineering higher education curricula (with reference to several fields such as Environment, Mechanic and ICT engineering).

Observatory on Engineers

The proposed project aims to meet needs identified in the wider policy imperatives set out in the Bologna Process, Lisbon Declaration and "New Skills for the New Jobs". The observatory will use regular surveys of engineers skills and competences to inform stakeholders with recommendations on matching skills supply and demand.

The engineering competence framework, based on EQF, provides the basis for the planned onterviews and the surveys. The investigations is addressed to industry, Engineering HE Institutions and individual engineers, focused on comparisons between competences developed from HE curricula and competences actually practiced at work, on recruitment policies and industry procedures.

The research completed to date has found that the main weaknesses of the graduates do not reside in the lack of technical skills, but mainly in insufficient development of managerial-organizational and linguistic skills.

Performance based assessment

Performance based assessment methods include portfolios, projects, coursework, reflective diaries, presentations, interviews, role-plays and group work. This approach has the advantages of:

- Increasing the range and 'real life' authenticity where learners are assessed.
- Incorporating more direct measures of attitudes in 'real-world contexts, such as observations.
- Capturing the learning processes and progression of learners in addition to the results of activities.

The University of Nottingham uses the Nottingham Advantage Award for Extra-Curricular Activities Programme to assess and recognize key competences acquired by students in non-academic contexts.

Nottingham Advantage Award For Extra-Curricular Activities

The University of Notthingham has introduced an Award to recognise extra-curricular achievements (like introduced an Award to recognise extra-curricular achivements (like sport, voluntary activities, work experience, learning a language, travel). Learning Outcomes have been defined so that the Award can provide formal recognition to students engaged in a range of extracurricular activities and develop a range of key employability (transferable) skills and competences.

Award modules combine experimential learning and reflective practice, offering students creative and practical ways to engage with the PDP (Personal Development Plan) process to enhance self-awareness, skills development and employablility. For instance, the "Career Planning Skills" module includes a series of training workshops that teach students how to effectively prepare for the recruitment process. Students are then assessed on their learning by taking part in a mock interview and completion of career profiling assessment.

Approximately 100 modules are being offered during 2012/13 including: Employability and Career; Enterprise, Events and Project Management; Study Abroad, Cultural Awareness and Language Learning; Volunteering and Work Experience.

Each module provides about 20 taught hours including: group workshops; online learning; virtual workshops and one-to-one tutorials. The remaining 80 notional hours include independent study and preparing evidence for the assessment which can be in wide variety of forms such as: posters; reflective journals; presentations; e-portfolios; workshops; essays; learning logs; video or pod casts and blogs or websites.

Peer and Self-assessment: portfolio and e-portfolio assessment

Self-assessment by the learner, with the support of teachers, assessors and peers, for the identification and management of their key competences is based on a "personal empowerment" approach (Duvekot, 2008). For a successful process of self-assessment, individuals need to: understand the intended learning outcomes and how evidence can be identified and collected while also be self-aware and engaged in personal development through reflection. The self-assessment or self-management of key competences contributes to formative assessment by: enhancing the capacity for individuals to manage their own development and the concomitant extension of the learners' self-efficacy to apply their learning processes across various contexts.

In a self-assessment process, the portfolio (or e-portfolio) becomes a key tool that allows individuals to identify, articulate and make explicit the learning results they have acquired in the University and other informal contexts. The portfolio methodology is a great opportunity for organisational innovation for teachers, trainers and employers, because it enables the planning of career goals in addition to its main functionality of the collection of evidences of personal skills.

The Centre for International ePortfolio Development (CIePD)[14] at the University of Nottingham has

14 See http://www.nottingham.ac.uk/CIePD/index.aspx

recently developed the Lifelong Learning Network (LLN) ePortfolio, which is described below.

The ePortfolio Lifelong Learning Network (LLN)

The Lifelong Learning Network (LLN) ePortfolio was developed at the Centre for International ePortfolio Development (CIePD) at the University of Nottingham and is configured as a system for the collection, recording and presentation of assessment as well as supporting the design of training and lifelong learning programmes and developing strategies for prefessional development. The LLN e Portfolio meets three main fuctions of supporting learning and development, assessment and presentation of competence.

The LLN ePortfolio has a space where individuals can share evidence of skills acquired and the rest of ePortfolio resources to external users such as employers. This tool also allows the application of external audit of the evidence of competences by academic tutors and mentors of the company who have access to the web platform.

6.2.6. E-assessment

There has been a steady increase in the use of e-assessment in universities including basic computer-based testing through to more complex forms of assessment, such as using augmented reality and immersive games. There is evidence that "embedding learning and assessment into computer simulations, virtual laboratories and computer games takes the learning process even further by enabling students to develop their scientific enquiry, analysis, interpretation and reflection skills by simulating real life contexts and repeatedly sampling performance" (EC Staff Working Document 371, 2012: 34).

6.2.7. Conclusion

The issues in the practice of assessment of Key Competences revolve around the notion that curricula changes are not reflected in changes in assessment practices where there is a tendency by those involved to focus on technical and subject specific competences rather than transversal Key Competences for learners. The challenges lie in making assessment methodologies more specific to capture learning which occurs outside formal settings. In light of the valuable examples in assessment of Key Competences at University level that have been discussed above, a combination of assessment approaches and methods is needed if a complete overview of acquired key competences and transversal competences is wanted. There is a need to focus on designing comprehensive strategies for the introduction of the assessment of key competences at university level in Europe. We present particular strategies for assessment further in the PROPOUND Action Plan.

This section provides a discussion of teaching and learning approaches in relation to developing Key Competences among postgraduate students at higher education institutions in Europe. The majority of pilot activities within the Propound project involved student self-assessment of competences but a few pilots included specific explicit planned teaching and learning interventions. The pilot activities by Fondazione Politecnico di Milano highlighted two aspects of learning from the pilot activities: firstly in terms of academic staff in terms of reflecting on transversal skills and Key Competences within their academic programmes and how these may be developed in students; secondly for students reflecting on their individual competence development and the nature of 'evidence' – what artefacts can be used to demonstrate competence. There is a wide range of methods of embedded teaching approaches available and specific examples are provided below.

6.3.1. Graduate Attributes Approach

The embedded approach to teaching is evident through the University of Edinburgh (UoE) Graduate Attributes framework that is implanted into degree programme specifications (DPS). Three overarching UoE Graduate Attributes (Enquiry and Lifelong Learning, Aspiration and Personal Development, Outlook and Engagement) are progressively developed through the University experience. These can be understood as a blend of four overlapping clusters or groups of skills and abilities that are tangible and cover skills and abilities associated with: Research and Enquiry, Personal and Intellectual Autonomy, Communication, and Personal Effectiveness. These are collectively referred to as the UoE Graduate Attributes framework and allow staff to reflect on the Graduate Attributes being instilled within degree programs.

The educational aims and programme outcomes made explicit in the Programme Specification document of any degree programme give rise to specific outcomes intended under the Graduate Attributes framework. The development of these graduate attributes is a constant throughout the University's learning, teaching and assessment. Applying these attributes to different contexts shapes students and graduates to academia (the type of students or researchers they can be), to society/community (the contribution to society and citizenship) and to work and career (their employability). It is these Graduate Attributes that help prepare students to tackle evolving challenges facing them at the end of their studies. In the context of work and career upon graduating, these Attributes impact the student's employability both in the short and long term. So, these attributes maximize the student's abilities to be successful and enhance their employability in a competitive labour market[15]. Hence the student experience is transformative by its nature and the development of these attributes is embedded into the teaching and learning methods deployed across University degree programmes.

15 UoE (2011) Graduate Attributes Explained, University of Edinburgh.

6.3.2. Graduate Competency Building

Similarly, in a report by the Estonian Qualifications Authority (EQA) on the work of the Estonian Business School (EBS) in enhancing students' employability, two Masters programmes make explicit the specific outcomes for graduates and the intended attributes (termed competences in this case) to be developed in students upon completion of the degree programmes through different approaches (teaching/training being one of them).

6.3.3. Work-based learning

Embedded teaching methods include students undertaking a workplace placement in an external organisation for a short period (e.g. one month). The focus of this course is on learning-by-doing involving personal theory building derived from experiential learning. The student is required to provide pieces of work for assessment as well as a report or presentation for the organisation in a form agreed through a learning contract. In such a learning and working environment, the student will, consciously or unconsciously, be developing their Key Competences. This is an innovative approach to achieving the graduate attributes via learning at work (experience) as a mode of delivery combined with formal assessment as part of the course.

The universities of Edinburgh, Aberdeen and Stirling are partners in the Making the Most of your Masters (MMM) project funded by the Scottish Funding Council as part of the Learning to Work Initiative. The initiative promotes collaboration between employers and higher education by providing postgraduate students with opportunities for work-based learning to enhance their employability and workplace relevant skills. MMM actively engages with employers to develop potential projects and dissertation topics as well as supporting appropriate workplace and academic supervision and development of documented project specifications and learning agreements. Evidence from the initiative found that employers engaged with MMM as a means for them to make a wider societal contribution, to take forward projects that they did not otherwise have the capacity to deliver, and to assist in research and development activities. Students participating in MMM report increased self-confidence in problem-solving and self-presentation and enhanced their personal professional development and understanding of the demands of the workplace.

6.3.4. Skills Workshops

There are a number of examples of explicit skills development workshops within or additional to existing academic programmes from the partners. For example, the University of Edinburgh's MSc in the Management of Training & Development includes skills workshops alongside the academic programme. These workshops are scheduled alongside the formal academic programme of study and are mandatory for students to attend but are not formally assessed or certificated nor do they carry any credits. Topics covered include: negotiation skills; project management; career planning; team building and group facilitation. The workshops were introduced to meet the requirements of the Chartered Institute of Personnel & Development (CIPD) who professionally accredit the programme, in terms of transversal skills development, experiential learning and enhancing self-awareness. The workshop topics are mapped to the CIPD's progression competence framework. The transversal skills of the professional human resource practitioner can be mapped to the Key Competences although this mapping has not been completed. The skills workshops also inform the student's approach to Personal/ Professional Development Planning and attitudes to lifelong learning. Academic staff as well as external practitioners deliver these workshops to enhance the 'authentic' nature of the learning experience for students. These skills workshops are supported by the provision online of self-assessment tools as well as links to other resources to support the transversal skills and Key Competence development of students.

However, experienced practitioners who are part-time students on the postgraduate programme tend not to attend the skills workshops. This is partly that as experienced practitioners taking the programme to validate and certificate existing experience and competence, they can already demonstrate and evidence the competences and skills required. Furthermore, the scheduling of the workshops is difficult for part-time as well as full-time students given the formers' other work and external commitments.

6.3.5. Blended and Online Teaching Approach

An online and blended approach to the development of key competences in postgraduate students can be seen in the example of the Fundación General Universidad de Granada Empresa (FGUGREM) pilot activities for the Propound project. In the FGUGREM pilot activities, the development of Key Competences took place in the context of a work-based learning component of a formal postgraduate programme and hence is situated within a formal learning context.

This is combined with the action-orientated focus of work-based learning that places an equal emphasis on both theory and experience through reflective learning, facilitated by a variety of approaches including an e-portfolio.

The direct teaching and learning approach makes explicit the nature of the Key Competences. As with other pilot activities in the Propound project, awareness-raising and reflective learning on transversal skills was assisted by the development and use of a specific assessment tool. A workshop was held to highlight the benefits of the recognition and development of individual key competences to inform self-awareness and enhance learner motivation. Furthermore, the Key Competences were highlighted in terms of employability by matching the demand from employers. The Key Competence development was delivered as an online skills workshop titled: "how to improve your presentation skills". Six students with an Academic Coordinator attended the two-hour workshop which involved a combination of standard Power Point presentations and online videos to illustrate the key messages along with practical exercises. A synchronous online delivery was selected along with an evening timeslot to provide the easiest access for the majority of students while also allowing for direct interaction between students.

Both skills workshops and online workshops as delivery approaches for ***competence specific training*** are easily transferable to many other specific higher education contexts. As an example, the University of Edinburgh**'s Institute for Academic Development** provide a range of specific skills workshops for postgraduate taught programme students specifically enabling development of the *Learning to Learn* competence including study skills and presentation skills. These are supplemented by asynchronous online learning courses such as the "eWriting online course" or on research data management (MANTRA). Also available are a series of e-resources including IT self-study workbooks and a bank of video clips of students talking about the challenges of postgraduate study and their particular approaches to note-taking, time management, and formal summative assessments.

6.3.6. Professional Development Portfolio Methods

Continuous professional development (CPD) or Professional Development Planning (PDP) is described as an essential component of the learning and development agenda for postgraduates and those beyond. This widely accepted practice is rooted in the idea that organisations shift the responsibility for personal development to the individual learner and see the ability to manage one's own professional growth as a key strength.

Professional Development Planning

CPD as a practice is encouraged within degree programs and this is evident in degree programmes like the previously mentioned MSc MTD and the MSc Human Resource Management (HRM) at the UoE. This arises through professional accreditation of the course with the Chartered Institute of Personnel and Development (CIPD), the UK's main professional body for those working in human resource development and management. The MTD Programme is validated by the CIPD while the MSc in HRM is currently in the process of seeking accreditation. The CIPD route for the MSc MTD enables students to complete the CIPD professional membership knowledge requirements. As part of this, the CIPD program requires that students maintain a Personal Development Plan (PDP) as part of their professional development, which should be completed at regular intervals. The PDP approach is not limited to the context of professional accreditation requirements but can be employed in less formal contexts and learning programmes. For example, the FGUGREM pilot intervention at Kandor Graphics as part of this project includes PDP by participating students as a mechanism for making existing competences more visible to the student and employer as well as identifying competence areas for further development. In addition, a PDP approach is compatible with and complementary to the Validation of Prior Learning (VPL) processes of the InHolland pilot activities.

E-Portfolio

E-portfolio items can be used for a range of activities in higher education and are commonly used in summative assessment through supporting the preparation and presentation of the evidence demonstrating competence. The FGUGREM pilot activities included the use of e-portfolios in the "self-management of key competences". E-portfolios can also clearly be used in supporting the transparent development of transversal skills in the context of formal academic programmes. A recent evaluative study at the University of Edinburgh on the use of e-portfolios in selection identified their use to provide structured exercises supporting self-directed learning (MSc Community Education) and reflective learning. An MSc in Advanced Nursing Studies used e-portfolios to enable students to develop transparent linkages between practice, academic work and lifelong learning.

6.3.7. Conclusion

The section provides an overview of examples of the range of teaching and learning methodologies and approaches in relation to developing Key Competences or transversal skills among postgraduate students in higher education institutions in Europe. The experiences of the Propound project to date suggest that the European Key Competences have a limited impact on the design and delivery of transversal skills development among postgraduate students. The teaching methodologies identified indicate that transversal skills development is mainstreamed within teaching methods and curricula design but that is less clearly made explicit to either students or staff. Enhancing awareness and understanding of the European Key Competences should provide an effective framework for a transparent approach to transversal skills development and models for how such skills can be developed. Furthermore, this raises questions on the implications for curricula design of enhancing the transversal skills development and Key Competences implementation at the postgraduate level.

6.4. Training the Trainers and Assessors

This section is a guideline for setting up nationally contextualized trainings for assessors. These contextualised trainings are targeted to those undertaking the assessment of key competences and the trainers and/or assessors in any given context can range from those in academic, administrative and strategic positions. The manual and the actual training modules are open to adaptation to any national/regional/local context.

6.4.1. Requirements for the trainer of assessors

A trainer who will train assessors of key competences should possess the following competences.

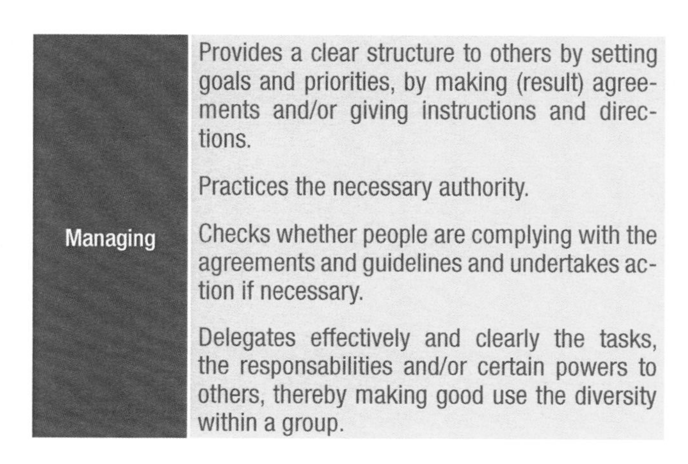

Managing	Provides a clear structure to others by setting goals and priorities, by making (result) agreements and/or giving instructions and directions. Practices the necessary authority. Checks whether people are complying with the agreements and guidelines and undertakes action if necessary. Delegates effectively and clearly the tasks, the responsabilities and/or certain powers to others, thereby making good use the diversity within a group.

Presenting	Is able to comment and explain the topics/subjects clearly, understandably and correctly. Communicates concisely and exudes confidence and expertise. Trains in an enthusiastic and inspiring way, with effective use of humor. Is emphatic to the audiences and works in a corresponding style of presentation.
Learning	Maintains their own expertise and skills if necessary and takes steps to further develop. Learns from mistakes and feedback. Demonstrates (actively and systematically) the working on own development.
Guiding	Coaches, advises and/or motivates others, aimed at achieving goals and/or performing of tasks and assignments. Empowers others to achieving results and solving problems (independently). Supports others actievely in their development.
Commitment and conviction	Makes a powerful and positive impression in the contact with others. Puts ideas and opinions forward with convincing arguments. Convinces also on the powerful direction to conversations, discussions and/or negotiations. Supports efforts to reach agreement on the outcome.
Applying professionalism	Knows, based on the own professionally/technical understanding, how to solve issues and problems. Shares, where appropriate, his knowledge and expertise with others.
Attention and understanding	Shows interest and understanding of the ideas, beliefs and emotions of others. Empathizes in the views and feelings of others. Listens well and demonstrates tolerance and kindness. Shows appropriate concern and support others when they have difficulties. Demonstrates self-reflection.
Ethics and integrity	Shows integrity and acts consistently in line with the norms and values of the organization, (professional) group and/or society. Takes into account the environment and respects differences between people.
Management of the needs and expectations of the "customer" (focus)	Investigates the needs and expectations of internal and/or external customers. Trying as much as possible to focus on these needs and expectations. Demonstrates a customer-friendly attitude. Keeps a close eye on the satisfaction of "clients" and takes action if necessary.

Besides controlling the aforementioned skills, the trainer of assessors needs to be able to function in different roles:

a) **Speaker:** In the training situation there is much interaction between the trainer and the group. There are also periods when the trainer has to explain issues in a more than one-dimensional manner.

b) **Leader:** Sometimes in a group there is a resistance to certain activities. The trainer is able to persuade them to act anyway.

c) **Coach:** When the trainer conducts an interview with an individual student, it is important that the trainer understands the strengths and weaknesses of that person. Listening is an important skill. Giving personal advice is the next step.

d) **Organizer:** Trainers are often also responsible for purchasing and coordinating training-programmes. In addition, there are often many practical issues concerning the training.

e) **Coach**: The trainer advises the client about the courses that are appropriate for solving the problems facing the client's organisation.

f) **Developer:** The coach is responsible for developing new courses. The trainer must be able to develop his own course material.

6.4.2. The competences of the assessor

Below is a description of the competences of an assessor:

Reviewing

The assessor is able to adequately provide an assessment of the competences of the participant, using a number of common competency-based assessment forms such as the portfolio, the criterion based interview and practical simulations. He can apply these assessment forms within a VPL procedure. The assessor is able to perform an assessment on the basis of a standard (competency-profile), to assess the provided evidence of the candidate on the basis of the prevailing assessment-criteria and to assess answers of a participant using the standard.

Observing

The assessor is able to adequately observe the participant and to link an assessment-report to this observation, in relation to the standard that was used as a basis for the assessment.

Interviewing

The assessor is able, by using specific questions and interview techniques in an assessment-situation, to make the competences of the participant transparent and to compare these competences in the interview with the standard. The assessor asks questions to investigate the value of the personal experiences (competences, knowledge and skills).

Providing feedback

The assessor is able to provide feedback to the participant in a constructive and motivating way and to indicate the results of the assessment, customized to the level of the participant.

The assessor can explain and substantiate the decisions based on the assessment and indicate at which points the participant is competent. N.B. only if this is part of the procedure, however, the guider may also do it.

Written communication

The assessor is able to write a clear, detailed and structured assessment report. The assessor describes the competences of the participant that are valid for the standard used. Personal characteristics are only added when applicable.

The assessor is technically competent and must have sufficient experience and qualifications in the appropriate discipline (professionally). The assessor can prove that he has sufficient technical skills and is willing to keep abreast of developments in the sector. The technical level of the assessor must be at least as high as that of the participant. The assessor is familiar with the assessment (VPL) procedure and objectives, the assessment tools and the methodology. The assessor is familiar with the sector or company standards (job descriptions, qualification profiles) and has knowledge of the labour market and vocational education programs for the sake of the assessment.

6.4.3. Design of the assessor training

In our Netherlands pilot, the basis of the assessor training consists of six modules, each with duration of half a day. The modular design allows, depending on the purpose and the experience of the target audience, to skip parts. A separate module is included for the guiders in Validation of Prior Learning (VPL) procedures.

Before the start of the training, the participants start with making their assessor-portfolio. This portfolio is complemented and updated regularly during the training (and after!) by the assessor-trainee. It may eventually serve as the basis for his or her certification as assessor. Between the training sessions the assessor-trainee performs training assignments.

After the training sessions the assessor-trainee receives a certificate of participation and is a candidate-assessor. Then the candidate-assessor - if the portfolio is complete and the candidate assessor has conducted enough assessments by him/herself – can complete the training with an external audit. A candidate-assessor has at least acted in two VPL procedures in the role of the second assessor (and/or guider). From that moment the candidate-assessor is eligible for the formal Assessor Certificate.

Chapter 7

Implications for Higher Education, Employers and Policy Makers

7.1. HE facing the learner's claim for fame

When facing the learner's claim for fame in HE in The Netherlands, the main implication is for understanding the shift in the nature of learning from a supply-steered orientation towards a 'partnership-in-learning' orientation of the learner, his/her working organisation and HE. In this partnership, VPL (or RPL) fills in the need for bridging prior learning and learning needs. VPL means for HE that individuals and organisations acquire a clear picture of their competency offers, demands and requirements, work on the formulation of their demands, and invest in their 'human capital'. The role of HE is primarily geared at updating and/or upgrading someone's personal learning biography for reasons of qualification, employability or empowerment.

For HE, VPL means acting as a 'listening' partner, initiating and offering VPL *and* custom work. The individual (employee or job-seeker) has to prepare him/herself or be prepared to explore, identify and develop his or her personal competencies so that he or she can work proactively on enhanced employability and further career development. VPL and custom work are outstanding tools with which the individual can attain this enhancement.

On the basis of desk-research and debates in stakeholder meetings, some general conclusions can be drawn:

1. VPL has everything to do with the use of the possibilities that lifelong learning has to offer to individuals and organisations in the fields of employability and empowerment. Organising responsibilities in VPL is a crucial part in this:

   a. The individual is in charge of putting together and maintaining the portfolio. The portfolio is the basis for the formation of a lifelong learning strategy.

   b. The organisation is responsible for defining the organisation's competence needs and to facilitate investment in its own *learning* employees.

c. The learning facilities (professional education, schooling and training) must be able to respond to the various learning needs of the learning individual, in other words be able to offer educational programmes that have been custom-made both structurally and in content.

2. There is support for the idea that the individual takes a central place in establishing, designing and implementing lifelong learning. This investment in human capital calls for co-makership of the learner him/herself. At all times the principal process here is the process of moving towards the desired learning goals, both when determining an individual's starting situation and during an individual's development course.

3. The portfolio is a powerful way to give structure and content to this co-makership. Guidance from within the labour market organisation could be a welcome push in this direction by offering:

   a. Training in self-management of competences. This is a useful way to start the formation of the desired portfolio.

   b. Help in putting together a portfolio in the work situation. An expert on the subject, easily approachable, who can offer help in designing a portfolio, is of great value in actually realising portfolio formation.

   c. Self-assessment tools, for instance, to help determine the competence and ambition level. This could be of great use in determining goals and direction in lifelong learning.

4. In the light of the different goals needed to make a start in lifelong learning, further research is needed into the motives for and the desired design of lifelong learning strategies. The variety of lifelong learning models (educational, upgrade, HRD and career models) can then be taken up on the basis of their own dynamics, in which the three actors (see 1a, b, c) can deal with varying responsibilities.

5. VPL as a bridge between the individual/organisation and professional education/schooling only becomes relevant when concrete learning questions have been formulated, which then need to be answered by professional education/schooling. The basis for all learning questions is, after all, deciding what the starting situation of the individual is. In addition, on the basis of a specific learning question a lifelong learning trajectory is offered; this could be a diploma trajectory but could also be enrichment learning in the form of modules, action learning, distance education, work guidance or otherwise.

6. VPL may serve as a bridge between the competence needs of the organisation and the individual. This calls for two forms of VPL:

   a. Synchronizing competence systems of labour market organisations on the one hand, with their competence management or HRM, and on the other hand schools and institutes, with their competence-focused curricula and training programmes. The goal of this synchronization is to determine which competencies and learning environments can be added to the portfolio; in this way the portfolio of the working individual can be fed and upgraded from within the HRM and the (professional) educational and schooling system. This form of VPL is top-down oriented and strives for a harmony between competence systems in the areas of supply and demand;

b. Through this synchronisation the learner can make clearer choices with regards to enriching his/her portfolio. The appreciation and recognition the learning individual seeks (partially dependent on the goals that have been set) can then be supported by two competence systems. VPL can provide concrete indications of what the most appropriate learning route for personal development is. In doing so, they can also make use of the competence acquisition that can be supported from within the own organisation or through external organisations. This form of VPL is bottom-up oriented VPL and looks for the balance between personal development questions and the most appropriate learning content and design.

7.2. Integrating key competences in learning outcomes

The main challenges and obstacles for integrating key competences in higher education practice can be identified as:

An assessment standard aiming at 'civil effect'. Assessment standards must meet the requirements of validity, acceptance, feasibility and functionality. Standards must be the 'property' of both the employer and employee. Correspondence with existing national qualification structures for vocational training should be sought. This offers the best possible assurance of the civil effects of qualifications acquired through prior learning assessment procedures, ranging from admissions to and exemptions from particular training courses, to further steps in the career development path. This will help education systems to open up and to respond quickly to required changes. For example, the design of standards for assessment is increasingly competence-driven. The standards are linked both to the competence requirements of professional practice and to the content of the supply of education and training. Cross-sector competences important to employability can also be defined. The capacity to define these assessment standards will also encourage the development of course-independent tests and examinations. The existing tests are rarely course-independent. Finally, the development of a recognition procedure for assessors creates confidence in the value of the accreditation procedure.

An important condition to create such an open situation is that the **standards** are **industry-driven**. The labour market should decide for itself which competences are required for accreditation as a practitioner in a particular profession. This relates not only to knowledge but also to skills and attitudes. In this case, the accreditation must be integrated into the corporate strategy. Only by focusing on formative goals, this usage of civil effect as a means and not an end in itself can be a powerful tool in turning learning into a lifelong learning facilitator of one's employability and empowerment.

Quality assurance of assessment procedures. In most countries, the government is directly or indirectly responsible for assuring the quality of the assessment standard. The quality of the standard can be controlled by establishing procedures for standard development and by using a programme of requirements for the design of standards (or qualification structures). The key quality criteria are validity, acceptance, functionality, transparency and comparability of structures.

The quality of VPL affects various parties with an interest in the assessment results. The government must supervise or regulate the quality (validity, reliability and fairness) of the assessment results. It can delegate these responsibilities to third parties, but remains answerable for quality supervision. The design of the quality assurance system could include an auditing of the assessment centres' internal quality assurance systems (as in the case of ISO certification), together with a system of random investigations of the validity and reliability of assessment results, conducted by independent research institutes. Criteria for the quality of assessment results can be drawn from the general requirements for assessment: validity and reliability. Naturally, both concepts must be operationalised specifically for prior learning assessment procedures.

Accessibility of procedures. Prior learning assessment procedures must be accessible to individuals and companies. Accessibility is determined by the recognition and acceptance of the accreditation. It is also determined by the accessibility of the organisations that implement the assessment procedures and their affordability. Access to competence recognition systems is determined by the features of the system itself and by the availability of financial resources. Decentralised supply of assessments increases the accessibility of the system. 'Decentralised' refers to the regional distribution of prior learning assessment and implementation of the procedures at the employee's place of work or training course.

Another condition for accessibility is that the system is workable and **efficient** for users. Time-consuming and bureaucratic procedures are disastrous to accessibility. The funding of prior learning assessment procedures is a fundamental condition for the use of the system. A decentralised and workable system that nevertheless costs the users too much will reduce access to the procedures.

7.3. For Employers

Transversal competences have always been crucial for employers, even when they do not enjoy such attention in public debate. Being a good employee does not deal only with the hard skills demonstrated and the theoretical preparation owned. Organizational, relational and communication skills are equally important to work productivity in a complex organization. Employers have for long complained about the inadequacy of university to equip students with needed competences.

In the knowledge society and in the present economic crisis such mismatch becomes just far more evident and critical.

Now more than ever, European companies are facing overwhelming challenges and are struggling to survive the present financial downturn and seek innovative ways to steer out of the crisis. European industry needs employees with more skills to be competitive, to be more responsive to changing demands, and require lifelong learning for its ageing workforce. The labour market is changing and so is the nature of occupations. There is evidence that there are rising skills requirement across all occupational groups from early elementary to high skilled jobs, especially in the fields of Health, ICT, Engineering, Sales and Finance.

The focus is on innovation, entrepreneurship, creativity, flexibility and change; they all point to advanced competences needed in individuals for them to take initiative, learn, solve problems autonomously, adapt to changing contexts, work in complex and multicultural environment, and contribute with quality and innovation in work processes.

In a context of instability and change, key competences of employees have therefore gained increasing importance in recruitment, selection and retention processes. Adding to this, financial and organisational constraints are faced by organisations in the training and development of new employees which challenge the integration of employees into the workplace. The era of globalisation, hyper competition and flatter organisational structures demands employees to be better managers, better organisers and effective learners who are focused on their professional development, and who will need ever increasing (and relevant) training and development.

In such a scenario, employers are wanting graduates with relevant (hence transversal) skills and competences. Employers and other labour market stakeholders are thus the ones who shall gain most from more employment oriented higher education programs. On this basis the European Commission in its communication "Towards a job-rich recovery" insists on "a better synergy between the worlds of education and work" such as the knowledge alliances to support investment in more relevant and better skills, including transversal ones.

The following can be considered short and long-term benefits that employers and companies can gain.

Facilitate full integration, autonomy and retention of new employees. First of all, with key competences effectively developed in post-graduate programmes, employers would be able to find "on the market" the competences and attitudes they normally would have to train and develop within their company, sharing efforts with Higher Education institutions.

In particular, more competent graduates would be an asset for employers since they would reduce cost and time for the company and thus lead to efficiency, quality, competitiveness and productivity. There is evidence of high failure rates within the first 18 months of taking a job caused by inappropriate attitudes and lack of key competences[i]. Improved training for key competences in undergraduate or postgraduate candidates can also reduce long term failure and in turn may improve employees' stability with the organisation.

This would lead instead to better integration and retention of employees who are expected to be autonomous and independent learners.

Redirect investment in training and learning. By sharing the responsibility of key competences training with higher education, employers can redirect their training and learning strategies to supporting the professional development of employees that is congruent with company objectives. Further to this, "Learning to Learn" is possibly the most important key competence which acts as the basis for the development of all other soft and hard skills. It guides systematic upgrading of competences within organisations and ensures a proactive attitude towards learning and change.

Therefore it has a pivotal role not only because it provides a self-sustaining momentum of learning, but also because learning provides satisfaction to employees that can enable a company to retain good employees.

Involve employees with shared innovation and development. Key competences are not intended as an "alternative" set of skills to the mere benefit of working process requirements. They also deal with the capacity of the individuals to orientate themselves in the labour market and with an organization, to make the best out of their skills and attitudes and contribute fruitfully with their actions. In this respect, investing more in developing key competences is expected to be favourable to the employer because employees will be willing to take responsibility and have proactive attitudes to work and their own development.

Have a say and participate in post-graduate programmes and career services. Employers have for long complained about the distance between HE programs and the competences they need. Increasing attention to key competences in post-graduate programmes by involving employers in their design and implementation would ensure that programme become labour market relevant and can encourage employability. Participation in post-graduate programmes will also permit employers to build long-term relationships with key higher education institutions that can prove worthwhile in many ways.

The benefits outlined above tie in with suggestions of the McKinsey Report findings that try to address the shortage of skills in the labour market[1]. These findings suggest that employers, education providers, and youth live in parallel universes where the education-to-employment journey is fraught with obstacles. Hence the education-to-employment system fails for most employers and young people and that the solution to this requires new incentives and structures. This is further elaborated in the next sub-section.

7.4. For Policy Makers

7.4.1. Education to Employment - Designing a system that works

There is a twin crises – a shortage of jobs (75 million unemployed young people in Europe, double that ratio in Euro zone) and a shortage of skills (similar number of entry level job vacancies) coupled with the lack of hard data specifying which skills are required for employment, what practices are the most promising in training youth to become productive citizens and employees, and how to identify the programs that do this best.

The McKinsey report's findings include the following six highlights:

1) **Employers, education providers, and youth live in parallel universes.** They have fundamentally different understandings of the same situation. Fewer than half of youth and employers, for example, believe that new graduates are adequately prepared for entry-level positions. Education providers, however, are much more optimistic: 72% of them believe new graduates are ready to work.

2) **The education-to-employment journey is fraught with obstacles.** The education-to-employment system is a highway with three critical intersections: (1) enrolling in postsecondary education, (2) building skills, and (3) finding a job. There are significant challenges at each intersection. At building skills, about 60% of youth say that on-the-job training and hands-on learning are the most effective instructional techniques, but fewer than half of that percentage are enrolled in curricula that prioritise those techniques. At finding a job, a quarter of youth do not make a smooth transition to work; their first jobs are unrelated to their field of study and they want to change positions quickly.

3) **The education-to-employment system fails for most employers and young people.** The survey identified three distinct groups of employers. Only 31% of employers are successful in getting the talent they require. They reach out regularly to education providers and youth, offering them time, skills, and money.

4) **Innovative and effective programmes around the world have important elements in common.** Two features stand out among all the successful programmes. First, education providers and employers actively step into one another's worlds. Employers might help to design curricula and offer their

employees as faculty, while education providers may have students spend half their time on a job site and secure them hiring guarantees. Second, employers and education providers work with their students early and intensely.

5) **Creating a successful education-to-employment system requires new incentives and structures.** To increase the rate of success, the education-to-employment system needs to operate differently, in three important ways:

   - Stakeholders need better data to make informed choices and manage performance. Parents and young people need data about career options and training pathways. All educational institutions should systematically gather and disseminate data regarding graduates' job-placement rates and career trajectory.
   - The most transformative solutions are those that involve multiple providers and employers working within a particular industry or function, especially on sector level.
   - Countries need system integrators (e.g. sector skills councils, qualifications agencies) responsible for taking a high-level view of the entire heterogeneous and fragmented education-to-employment system. The role of the system integrator is to work with education providers and employers to develop skill solutions, gather data, and identify and disseminate positive examples. Such integrators can be defined by sector, region, or target population.

6) Education-to-employment solutions need to scale up. There are three challenges to achieving scale:

   - Constraints on the resources of education providers, such as finding qualified faculty and investing in expansion.
   - Insufficient opportunities to provide youth with hands-on learning.
   - The hesitancy of employers to invest in training unless it involves specialized skills.

There are solutions for each challenge:

- Coupling technology (the Internet and other low-cost outlets) and a highly standardised curriculum can help to supplement faculty and spread consistent instruction at a modest cost.
- Apprenticeships traditionally have provided hands-on experience, but there are not enough spaces to meet demand. Technology, in the form of "serious games" and other kinds of simulations, can help here too, by offering tailored, detailed, practical experience to large numbers at a comparatively low cost.
- Employers often are willing to invest only in those specialized skills whose value they can fully capture; they do not want to spend money on employees who might take their expertise elsewhere. But for providers, it is expensive to develop solutions for every employer. One proven approach is to combine customization and scale by offering a standard core curriculum complemented by employer-specific top-ups.

CONCLUSIONS

Chapter 8

Conclusions

The main objective of the PROPOUND project has been to promote curricular reforms directed to improve the employability potential of postgraduate students. The project has attempted to encourage dialogue and cooperation between the universities and enterprises for the exchange and design of innovative curricular strategies and tools in postgraduate programmes that can better respond to the labour market needs and promote the development, assessment and certification of the key competences of postgraduate students.

The project has attempted to develop, experiment with and validate different methodologies for the identification and evaluation of Key Competences in postgraduate programmes across Europe. In reviewing the European context and the drive to meet the needs of the wider labour market, we have reviewed relevant policy, institutional and legal matters that bid to strengthen the employability potential of their young highly qualified graduates by improving educational attainment levels and by introducing necessary key competences in curricular programmes. We find that despite this wealth of policies, processes and strategies, the European Key Competences Framework remains largely unknown and unimplemented in most European universities.

We find that the focus for Key Competences is on entry to education or entry to the workforce. There is little attention to key competences in higher education, even less so at post-graduate level, despite the relentless complaints from employers over many years that graduates and post-graduates are less than work-ready. This may be because universities are structured along traditional subject lines, and academic staff are recognised and rewarded for their subject related work rather than the employability of their students.

On the whole, one of the key success factors for including key competences in the formal recognition process is consensus within the university communities of teaching staff and students as well. Hence, the first step is deciding together that key competences are to be formally recognised. The project recommends two possible routes for Key

Competences formal recognition as discrete and embedded.

With reference to assessment methodologies, the practice of assessment of Key Competences evolve around the notion that curricula changes are not reflected in changes in assessment practices while there is a tendency by those involved to focus on technical and subject specific competences rather than transversal key competences for learners. There is a need to focus on designing comprehensive strategies for the introduction of the assessment of Key Competences at university level in Europe.

In relation to teaching and learning methodologies and approaches in relation to developing Key Competences or transversal skills among postgraduate students in higher education institutions in Europe, the experiences of the Propound project to date suggest that the European Key Competences have a limited impact on the design and delivery of transversal skills development among postgraduate students. The teaching methodologies identified indicate that transversal skills development is partly mainstreamed within teaching methods and curricula design but that is less clearly made explicit to either students or staff.

Enhancing awareness and understanding of the European Key Competences should provide an effective framework for a transparent approach to transversal skills development and models for how such skills can be developed. There are vast challenges to be addressed and these challenges have implications for higher education, employers and policy makers. The solutions to these challenges lie in the very nature of all three working together in reforming higher education curricula and methods for the development of key transversal competences in graduates for better graduate employability in the EU labour market.

Authors:

Fundación General Universidad de Granada Empresa

Carmen Osuna López mcosuna@fundacionugrempresa.es
Marina Manzano Fernández mmanzano@fundacionugrempresa.es

Scienter CID

Petra Sulovska psulovska@scienter.es
Teresa Navarro tnavarro@scienter.es

Stiching Hoger Onderwijs Nederland-Hogeschool Inholland

Ruud Duvekot Ruud.duvekot@inholland.nl

Foundazione Politecnico di Milano

Clementina Marioni Clementina.marioni@fondazione.polimi.it

Scienter SOC. CONS. a RL

Monica Turrini mturrini@scienter.org
Daniela Proli dproli@scienter.org

Cambridge Professional Development

Nigel Lloyd NigelL@camprof.com
John O´Sullivan 101642.2113@compuserve.com

University of Edinburgh

Peter Evans peter.evans@ed.ac.uk
Ally Memon A.R.Memon@sms.ed.ac.uk

Sihtasutus Kutsekoda

Olav Aarna Olav.aarna@kutsekoda.ee